make it green

Unforgettable TOTE BAGS

20 DESIGNS TOO COOL TO LEAVE IN THE CAR

Eleanor Levie & Celebrity Quilters

"This book will guide you through putting your own creative voice on your reusable shopping bags. Make carrying your own bags a really important way of showing the world who you are, while you help heal the Earth!"

—SUSAN SHIE, OUTSIDER DIARY ART QUILT PAINTER

D1404160

Unforgettable Tote Bags
First in a *make it green* series
Copyright Eleanor Levie, 2009

Published by Eleanor Levie
Craft Services, LLC
259 Cherry Lane
Doylestown, PA 18901-3112
www.EleanorLevie.com

ISBN-10: 0615317502

ISBN-13: 978-0-615-31750-2

All rights reserved: Permission is granted to the retail purchaser to photocopy patterns for personal use only. No part of this product may be reproduced in any form for commercial use without the express and written permission from the author/ publisher.

Notice of liability: Every effort has been made to ensure that this book is complete and accurate. The information in this book is presented in good faith, but no warranty is given nor results guaranteed. Since we have no control over choice of materials or procedures, neither Eleanor Levie nor Craft Services, LLC can assume any liability or responsibility for the use of this information.

Author and Publisher:
Eleanor Levie, www.EleanorLevie.com

Cover & page designer:
Lesley Weissman-Cook, allshookup@comcast.net

Photography for all full page images:
Donna H. Chiarelli Studio, www.dhcstudio.com

Associate editor:
Valerie Egar, v873@hotmail.com

Review editor:
Nancy Breland

Photo-stylist:
Molly Rosenquist, mollyrosenquist@gmail.com

Illustrators:
Rachel Shelburne, rachel@sdr0.com
Joseph John Clark/Pubtech, LLC

Technical wizardry:
Jacob Cook

Printer:
Barefoot Press, Raleigh, NC, www.barefootpress.com, a green printer since 1987, committed to eco-friendly printing with soy ink on recycled paper

Acknowledgments

Heaps of gratitude to Carl Harrington, marketing guru and unforgettable wordsmith, stress mitigator, clever troubleshooter, and darling husband.

Kudos to our son, Sam Levie Harrington, who inspired this book. An innovative environmental designer and engineer, he is living his dream and saving the planet. A mother couldn't be more proud.

Lesley Weissman-Cook has my appreciation, untold, told and retold, for her forbearance with me and with the process, and for her ever-conscientious attention to detail and great design.

Thank you, Donna H. Chiarelli (and techie Tom Wolfe!) for giving me, as always, beauty-ful photos endowed with sense and sensibility.

Hooray for Valerie Egar, Nancy Breland, and Rachel Shelburne—unstinting advocates for the rights of the reader to clear, accurate text and illos (illustrations).

To Molly, Anna, Jack, Buddy, Rudy Mink, and Natalie—Good-looking and good-humored, patient and poised—you rock!

Nonesuch Farm Store in Doylestown, PA, my favorite place to food shop: You were all so gracious in allowing our camera crew to disturb the tranquility of your charming market.

Eternal indebtedness to all the quilting stars who generously shared their time and talents to participate in this book. They readily said yes to my invitation, went in with no holds barred, and gave me everything I dreamed of and more. I'm so happy to count you as friends.

Contents

Introduction

What's the biggest obstacle to using cloth bags when you do your food shopping?

No matter who gets asked this question, the answer is always the same: "I forget to bring them in from the car." Sound familiar? We all *want* to cut down on plastic and paper bags. We all *want* to do our share to reduce our carbon footprints. But . . . **we just can't remember those bags.**

So the idea for this book was hatched: Showcase fresh, inspirational designs to entice quilters and do-it-yourselfers to make or personalize bags so interesting and attention-grabbing that you won't forget about using them.

First order of business was asking top quilters to apply their talents and signature styles to this challenge, and I was thrilled at the very big stars—all extremely busy with teaching and commissions—who readily said, "Count me in!" Second, I added my own designs to round out the bunch of projects and ensure there's something for everyone. Third, I hired one of the first green printers, here in the USA. In fact, everyone on my team had an eye for

quality and style, and an interest in making this book eco-friendly as well as user-friendly.

The end result, which you hold in your hand, is divided into three main sections. *On the Fast Track* includes designs that all begin with a ready-made bag, an idea that originated with Karen Eckmeier in her *Layered Waves* book, and was re-engineered in various ways. The second section, *Sew Simple,* offers several easy bag constructions and clever designs. I call the third section *Play with Paint,* and here's where everyone can be an artist, and have fun, too. At the back of the book, there is a *Bag Basics* feature with info on cutting and stitching and customizing for comfort and convenience. A *Resources* section makes it easy to get hold of all the materials and tools these quilt stars like to use.

Consider making a gusseted Fine Feathered Bag with Log Cabin rounds like the Nona bag, or appliqués taken from the UnBeetable design, adding rounded tube handles like the Seminole Inspiration. You get the picture: mix and match features at will, bringing in ideas from other parts of the book . . . or even better, your own creative whims!

No matter what your taste or which techniques you enjoy, you're sure to find a design that's **downright unforgettable.** No matter how time-crunched you are, there are projects here that take as little as an hour. No matter how timid you are about trying something new, the pressure is off: It's not fiber art, a best-of-show wannabee, or a commemoration of a major event . . . it's *just* a tote bag. Wherever you carry it, no one is gonna notice the little glitches. But it will earn you compliments on your exquisite taste, show you care about planet Earth, inspire others to do their share . . . **and make you remember to take your unforgettable tote bags into the store in the first place!**

Enjoy getting tote-ally creative!

Elly

Eleanor Levie

On the
FAST TRACK

Feeling a time crunch? A ready-made bag gives you a head start, so you can whip up your creation in the morning, and go shopping that same day. Extra-sturdy construction for substance and style!

Pour On the Color

by Judy Hooworth

ONE OF AUSTRALIA'S BRIGHTEST QUILT STARS proves that going green needn't restrict your use of color! Judy Hooworth combined small amounts of eye-popping solids, because, as she says, "Bright colors celebrate all that is joyous in life; they make me feel good!" However, you may wish to use pale and medium tones, or just two different colors, or whatever your heart desires. No matter your palette, a smart black and white stripe and easy-to-piece sawtooth squares are guaranteed to add flavor. Judy cleverly used a plain tote bag as a sturdy lining for her patchwork. While there may not be a pot of gold at the end of this rainbow-hued tote bag, there're sure to be rewards—gallons of compliments on your eco-conscious style!

What you'll need

Dimensions: 19" x 15" x 7" deep

- 1 large canvas bag (this one from SewNeau; see Resources on page 61); for other sizes, adjust all measurements as needed

- Fabrics:
  ⅔ yard of black
  ½ yard black and white stripe
  Fat eighth of white
  3½" x 13" strip from each of 12 assorted colors

- ¼ yard fusible web

- 12 red ¾" sew-thru buttons

Cutting

From black and white striped fabric:
   Place 45° angle on ruler along bottom edge of black and white stripe. Cut strips on the bias: two 3½" x 22½" and two 4½" x 22½".

From black fabric, cut across width of fabric:
   One strip 7½" wide. Cross-cut to get rectangles: one 7½" x 20" and one 7½" x 12½"

   One strip 4" x 38½"
   One strip 1½" x 31". Cross-cut to get 2 strips 1½" x 15½"

From each solid color, cut:
   One strip 3½" x 13". Cross-cut to get two 3½" x 6½" rectangles, for a total of 24

From white, cut:
   One strip 7½" x 20"

From fusible web, cut:
   Two strips 2¾" x 22½", and two strips 4¼" x 20"

Double sawtooth strips

1 Press the 7½" x 20" black and white strips with spray starch and then press them together, aligning all edges carefully. Cut the paired strips lengthwise into thirds to get three 2⅜" x 20" strips. Cross-cut each of these paired strips into eight 2⅜" squares.

2 With the white square on top, lightly pencil a diagonal line as shown on the next page. Stitch ¼" seams to either side of the marked line, then rotary-cut along the penciled line. Flip the units so the black side is on top. Press to set the stitches, then press the black triangle open

so seam allowances are pressed toward the black fabric. Trim the dog ears. In this way, make 48 triangle squares.

3 To make sawtooth strips, join squares in pairs using ¼" seams. Join pairs to make 4 rows of 12 squares. Join rows together in pairs to make 2 double sawtooth strips.

Rainbow patchwork

1 Make two piles, each with a 3½" x 6½" rectangle from each of the 12 colors. Using first pile, arrange different-color rectangles into 2 rows of 6; refer to photo of bag on page 7. Using ¼" seams, stitch each set of rectangles together along their long edges to form the rainbow patchwork. Press seam allowances in one direction, or as needed to prevent shadow-through. Repeat using the second pile. Be sure to arrange the colors so that each side of bag features the full assortment of fabrics.

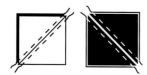

Take time for texture

Layer the rainbow patchwork and sawtooth strips over a thin piece of batting, and quilt diagonal rows or a grid, or letters for a name or monogram.

2 Pin one rainbow patchwork from the first pile along its joined edge to the top edge of a double sawtooth strip. Match seams where possible, then stitch. Join the other rainbow patchwork from the first pile to the bottom of the double sawtooth strip to complete the patchwork section. Press seam allowances toward the black fabrics. Repeat for the second pile.

Rim

1 Using a seam ripper, remove the handles on the tote.

2 Trim the two 4½"-wide striped fabric strips to measure ½" larger than width of bag. Join the strips together at each end, making a loop. Press seams open, then press one long edge ¼" to the wrong side.

3 Press the 4¼"-wide fusible web to the wrong side of each strip in the loop, covering the folded edge. Remove the paper backing.

4 Turn tote inside out. With a pencil, mark a line 1¾" from top edge. With wrong sides together and matching side seams, pin folded edge of loop along pencil line. Next, fold striped fabric over the rim of tote to the right side. Press, removing pins as you go. Then, working from the inside, topstitch along the ¼" folded edge of the striped fabric, through all layers.

Assembly

1 Sew a black 1½" x 15½" strip to each side of the rainbow patchwork and double sawtooth strips unit. Press seam allowances toward the black strips.

2 Pin these two units (front and back of bag) together, right sides facing, and stitch along the sides with the black strips to form a cylinder. Press seam allowances to one side.

3 To attach the bottom of the bag, pin the 7½" x 12½" black rectangle along the bottom edge of the rainbow patchwork section, with wrong sides together and

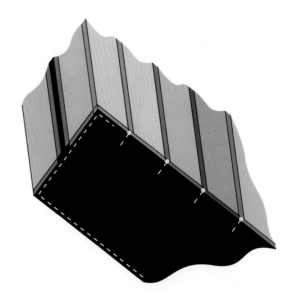

Judy Hooworth

New South Wales, Australia

Traditional and contemporary: Judy Hooworth has earned international acclaim and dual citizenship in both quilt worlds. She revels in color, and her modern take on patchwork traditions has been showcased in three books, *Razzle Dazzle Quilts, Spectacular Scraps,* and *Quilts on the Double.* As a fiber artist, Judy creates works of tiered and painted cotton that reflect the views of water, trees, and birds outside her window. Her masterworks have been featured four times in Quilt National, the most respected juried show for art quilts. A former art teacher, Judy now helps students develop their patchwork, quilting, and personal vocabulary for art quilts.

centering the seams of the black strips along the short sides of the black rectangle. Stitch together, backstitching at the start and end for reinforcement.

4 Measure around the top edge of the bag, add ½", and trim the 4" x 38½" black strip to that length. Sew the ends together to make a loop, and press seam allowances open. With right sides together, pin this strip to the top edge of the patchwork bag; align seams on one side of the tote. Sew together, then press toward the black strip. At this point, the pieced bag lacks only the rim.

5 Turn pieced bag right side out. Test-fit the bag on the canvas tote, and mark a foldline 1" from upper edge—or as needed to overlap the striped rim by at least ¼". Press hem along fold line to wrong side.

6 Insert canvas tote (handles previously removed) wrong side out into the outer pieced bag. Align side and bottom seams. Turn the folded edge of the black fabric at the top 1¼" from top edge of tote, and pin in place. Also pin along all horizontal seams.

7 Topstitch on the folded edge of the black material, sewing through the striped fabric and the canvas tote.

Finishing

1 Stitch in the ditch along all horizontal seams on the bag (a cinch if your machine has a free arm!).

2 Refer to the Bag Basics on page 63 to wrap handles with remaining 3½"-wide striped strips. Pin the ends of one handle to the bag front, centered and 10½" apart. Secure with a boxed criss-cross. Repeat with the second handle on the bag back.

3 Measure and mark button placements on black strip at the top of the bag, so that buttons will be evenly spaced, 6 on each side of the back. Sew buttons securely through all layers. 🍂

Make embellishments your bag

Buttons are just one way to decorate this plain band. Consider charms, ribbon, rickrack, a hand-embroidered name or saying, a machine-stitched monogram . . . or several elements in combination.

The Nona Bag

by Kaffe Fassett & Liza Prior Lucy

"THE YEAR BEFORE MY GRANDMOTHER DIED," writes Kaffe Fassett about his "Nona," *"she gave me a gorgeous Middle Eastern embroidery of rich pink, yellows, limes, and black silk geometry. Before I could properly enjoy it, it was stolen from me, but the memory had burnt into my mind."* Thirty years later, Kaffe found expression for his reverie in his Nona quilt, translated into cloth by Liza Prior Lucy and featured in the book, Passionate Patchwork (see page 13). And ten years after that, Kaffe and Liza revisit the charming, free-form Log Cabin design, putting it on a big shopping tote.

Liza is passionate about keeping projects like this simple—even for rank beginners. It's fast, because it uses the front of a ready-made bag as a foundation for a single large block, and builds out from the center with just a few scraps and seams with no measuring and no fuss. And, it's fresh, reinterpreted with Kaffe's new fabrics. Make one for you, one for your mom, and one for your Nona!

What you'll need

Dimensions: 19" x 15" x 7" deep

- 1 large canvas bag (this one from SewNeau*); for smaller sizes, reduce the number of fabrics, as you'll need fewer rounds of logs

- Fabric: Scraps to ¼ yard each of 8-10 different prints, including one large scale floral for the center. Fabrics, designed by either Kaffe Fassett or Philip Jacobs,* are as follows, starting from the center: Zinnia in pink, Aboriginal Dots in lime, Kirman in orange, Spot in magenta, Lake Blossoms in yellow, Spot in peach, Henna in yellow, Tropical in pink, Clover in orange.

- Ecru sewing thread

*See Resources on page 61

Cutting

From large scale floral fabric, fussy-cut a flower for the center, about 3½" square . . . but not a perfect square, and need not be on grain.

From the other fabrics, cut strips across the longest edge, approximately 1" to 2½" wide. Do not try to cut them accurately—just use a straight-edged ruler and make a slice.

Preparing the bag

1 Cut along side seams, or use a seam ripper to open both sides of the bag.

2 If your bag has a boxed bottom, rip out to the corners to release just the front, so it flaps out loose from the sides, yet is still attached at the bottom. See photos on next page.

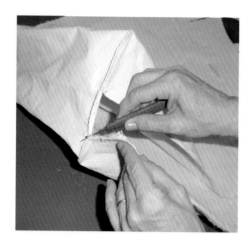

Build the block

1 Locate the center of the tote front and pin on the fussy-cut square, right side up. If perfection is your thing, you can fold and crease the bag front and fabric square and match the creases to align this patch and all the logs. If, on the other hand, you lean toward the charmingly offbeat, simply plop it down *somewhat* centrally.

Cue for the askew!

Is liberated liveliness your bag? Why not set the center square on a much more wonky angle, as shown above, and kick it off center, to boot.

2 Choose a strip of fabric for the first log. Place one end of the strip right side down on top of the center square so that the edges are even on one side. Stitch ¼" from that edge.

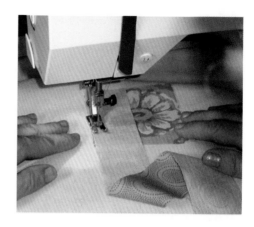

3 Fold the fabric strip to its right side and press. Trim the ends of the strip so they are flush with the edges of the center square. Take the strip you've trimmed and, moving clockwise, position it along the adjacent edge. Sew, press, and trim as before. Repeat two more times, to make one round.

4 Choose another fabric and sew another round in the same way. Continue with rounds of different fabric strips until the fabric extends beyond the bag edges on the sides and bottom but doesn't overlap the hem and ends of the bag handles at the top.

Finishing

1 Trim the sides even with the tote. Trim the block edges on the top and bottom, leaving ¼" to ½" to turn under. Turn, press, and topstitch these edges to the bag.

2 Fold the bag crosswise in half, with right sides in. Re-stitch the side seams, slightly to the inside of the previous stitching. Clean-finish the seam allowances with zigzag stitching. With bag still wrong side out, stitch the bottom corners to restore the boxed bottom. Press.

Kaffe Fassett & Liza Prior Lucy

Kaffe Fassett and Liza Prior Lucy have been design partners since 1990, creating quilts and writing books that showcase these rich textile collaborations. Kaffe, born and raised in California, has long called London, England home. He is a painter whose color sensibilities translate into patchwork and appliqué thanks to quiltmaker Liza Prior Lucy, who lives in Bucks County, Pennsylvania (not far from where I live!). Liza's online fabric shop (www. GloriousColor.com) specializes in selling fabric designed by Kaffe and other contemporary talents.

Passionate Patchwork *introduced the Nona quilt, a forerunner of this tote design.*

What's for Dinner?

by Karen Eckmeier

THAT UNIVERSAL QUESTION heard by every family cook is the inspiration and title of Karen Eckmeier's sassy supermarket bag. A prolific designer and author, Karen invariably cooks up new recipes for quilting. In fact, she introduced this cool way to alter ready-made cloth bags, rather than make them from scratch. Here, she uses photo-transfer to create her own fabric, jam-packed with eco-slogans. "I'm reminded to try new recipes and to think <u>green</u> as I'm food-shopping," says Karen, "and in a gentle way I am signaling to others my high standards for the foods I buy for my family, and the fact that I care enough about the earth to use a recyclable bag." You go green, girlfriend!

What you'll need

Dimensions: 19" x 15" x 7" deep

- 1 large canvas bag (this one from SewNeau*); for other sizes, adjust measurements as needed

- Fabrics:
  Six 8½" x 11" fabric photo transfer sheets*
  ½ yard black for top border, squares, accent stripes and handle wraps
  ¼ yard white for squares
  ⅛ yard small-scale black-and-white checkerboard print for top border/inside flap
  ¼ yard large-scale vegetable print for accent blocks

- 4 red 1" sew-thru buttons

- 1 button with frog loop for top closure (optional)

*See Resources on page 61

Cutting

Open up the bottom and side seams (see Bags Reborn, page 20). Cut off the handles even with the top of the bag and set aside.

From black fabric, cut:
  2 strips 2½", selvage to selvage
  4 strips 2" x 18½"
  2 strips 3½" x 17½" (or length of handle + 1")
  2 strips 2" x 6½"

From white fabric, cut:
  2 strips 2½", selvage to selvage

From checkerboard print, cut:
  2 strips 3½" x 18½"

From large-scale vegetable print, cut:
  2 rectangles 6½" x 9"

Text sections

1 Referring to the designs shown here and on page 16 (which were found on Macintosh clipart), create your own text and symbols on your computer, using various font styles and sizes. Print out on 8½" x 11" paper.

2 Photocopy "What's for Dinner?" and "Eat Your Veggies!" each centered onto a photo-transfer sheet. Keeping the text centered, cut into 6½" squares.

Text-messaging, the easy way!

*Add lettering with alphabet rubberstamps or stencils
and fabric ink, or work freehand with fabric markers.*

3 Photocopy multiple slogans onto four photo-fabric
sheets. With text centered, cut four 6½" x 9" rectangles.
Using ¼" seams, stitch them together in pairs to make
two 6½" x 17½" text rectangles.

Black and white checks

1 Cut the black 2½" strips into 21 squares. Cut the white
2½" strips into 24 squares.

2 Arrange 7 squares in a row, starting with a white
square and alternating with black. Join, using ¼" seams.
Press toward the black. Repeat 3 times to make 4 units.

3 For the center of bag, arrange 17 squares in a row,
starting with a black square and alternating with white.
Stitch and press as before.

Assembly

1 Stitch one 2" x 18½" black strip to each side of the
3½" x 18½" checkerboard print strip. Repeat, to make 2
units. Press seam allowances toward the checkerboard
print on both units.

2 Arrange units as shown below. Take care to orient the
text and veggie print correctly for the front and back.

3 Join a 6½" x 17½" text section, a veggie print, a 2" x
6½" black strip, and an upside-down 6½" text square.
Press seam allowances toward the darker pieces.
Repeat, to make 2 text/veggie units.

4 Pin and stitch between the text/veggie units, easing
to fit as necessary. Press seam allowances towards the
text/veggie units. Then, stitch a row of 7 checks flush with
each corner, as shown in the exploded diagram at left.
Finally, join a pieced border to either end.

5 Lay the opened bag out flat on a work surface, wrong
side up. Center the pieced design on top, and pin in
place. Using black thread and beginning at the center and
working outward, stitch in the ditch (right on the seam)
between units.

6 Turn the edges of the black border strip under, even
with the rim of the bag. Topstitch to secure. Trim the
sides of the bag to match the width of your pieced top.
Reassemble, following Reconstruction, on page 20.

Karen Eckmeier

Kent, Connecticut
www.quilted-lizard.com

Karen brings her warmth, energy, and sense of whimsy to quilters in her popular workshops and publications. So it was no accident that the ways she developed for cutting and topstitching curves made her book, *Accidental Landscapes,* wildly successful. Her next and most recent book, *Layered Waves,* applies the same techniques to accessories as well as quilts. Shown here are two market bags featured in that book, plopped down on Karen's kitchen counter. Karen laughs as she shares her secret— "I didn't know how to make a bag, so I just figured out a way to kind of cheat and use an existing one." So NOT cheating, Karen! Your super-easy shortcut impressed me so much, I had to showcase it in this book. Previous pages show how Kaffe and Liza applied this method to one side of a bag only. And on the next pages, you'll see how I used it to make three bags full of raw-edge texture.

7 Referring to Bag Basics on page 63, cover the canvas handles you removed and set aside with black fabric.

8 To create a flap, fold half of the top border of the bag to the inside of the bag, leaving only half of the checkerboard print showing along the top edge of the bag. Position the ends of one handle on the inside black border strip, centered on the front of the bag and 4½" apart. Pin in place without catching the flap. Unfold the border and secure handles with a boxed criss-cross (see Bag Basics, page 63).

Finishing

1 Stitch a red button to each end of both handles.

2 To prevent goodies from spilling out of your bag, stitch a button and frog loop to the center of the top edges. 🍂

Get into the Fray

by Eleanor Levie

THESE ESSENTIAL ECO-TOTES start with plain canvas bags in one of the most planet-friendly fabrics you can get: natural, undyed, organic 100% cotton. Open the side seams to flatten each bag, and then stitch on shapes cut from a similar fabric. Each easy-going project features random curves, repeat triangles, or stacked squares, but you can stitch on any strip or concentric shape that floats your boat or drives your car! Aim to do a lot of cutting on the bias and leave those fabric edges raw. Every time you wash these bags, the design areas fray a little more and the texture really revs up. And since each of these designs is super quick, you can sew up all the super-sized sacks your shopping trips demand.

What you'll need

Dimensions: 19" x 15" x 7" deep

- 1 large canvas bag for each (these from SewNeau; see Resources on page 61); for other sizes, adjust measurements as needed

- ¼ yard of natural canvas (duck) fabric for each

- Taupe thread, 30 weight, plus 50 weight for the bobbin

How-to's for all

1 Pre-shrink bag and follow directions for Deconstruction on page 20.

2 To add texture to your bag, use the thicker 30-weight thread in the top of machine, and standard 50-weight sewing thread in the bobbin.

3 Reassemble the bag; see Reconstruction on page 20.

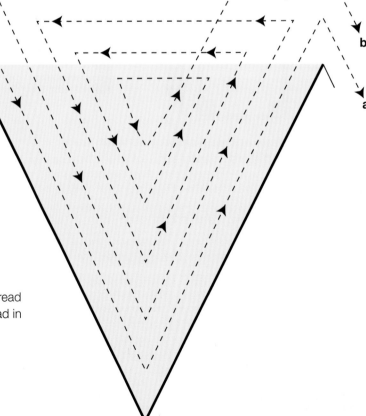

Bags Reborn

Here's how to open up a ready-made bag, so you can have a flat piece to work on before reassembling the bag. What an easy way to take a tote from ho-hum to humdinger!

Deconstruction

1 Prewash bag in hot water and dry on hot to pre-shrink. Steam-press to produce a smooth, wrinkle free surface for doing your foundation piecing or appliqué work.

2 Turn bag wrong side out. In most cases, the seam allowances are narrow and serged, or even bound. Though you'll lose a little width, it's best to simply trim them off using sharp scissors.

3 If your bag features a simple, boxed bottom (directly below), use a seam ripper to carefully take out stitches from the bottom of the side seam to each bottom corner. Open out the bag's front and back and lay flat on the table. You'll notice rectangular cut-outs along the middle of the long edges.

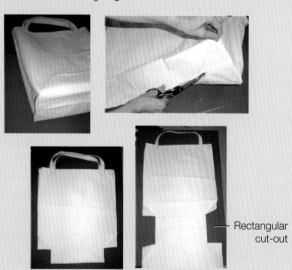

— Rectangular cut-out

4 If your bag features a triangular fold ("tent-tuck") at the bottom of each side, turn bag wrong side out. Notice that side seams are straight, with no cut-out boxes. Because the bottom is boxed without cut-outs, this type of construction tends to make the bag a bit stronger. However, there are four layers of canvas at the bottom of the side seams on each side.

A Note of Caution: To reconstruct this type of bag, your sewing machine must be able to penetrate 4 layers of canvas. See Canvassing the Joint, page 62, for tips.

With such thick bulk to cut through, use spring-action scissors (as shown above) or use a long acrylic ruler and a rotary cutter with a large blade (60mm) to trim off the side seams.

Reconstruction

1 Fold the bag crosswise in half, with right sides in.

2 For all stitching, sew ¼" from the edges. Then, stitch again ⅛" from edges to reinforce the seam, and clean-finish the seam allowances with zigzag stitching. If you have a serger, you can surge through this step in no time.

3 If your bag has a cut-out square in the bottom corners, leave the bag wrong side out. On the boxed cut-out at the bottom of each side, stretch out tautly the two opposite corners that are not above the side seam. Pin, stitch, and re-stitch as indicated in step 2 above. Then turn the bag to the right side and press.

4 If you are restoring tent-tucks at the bottom, pin along each side edge: at the very bottom, and 3" above—which will result in a bag that is 6" deep. Adjust these measurements for a narrower or wider base. Bring pins together to create an inside pleat. Stitch along both side edges as indicated in the previous step. Press, turn bag to right side, and press again.

Tent-tuck —

Rag Zigzag Bag

1 Trace or photocopy the tan actual-size triangle pattern on page 19. Glue to cardboard and cut out template.

2 Fold canvas crosswise in half (as it comes off the bolt). Referring to the diagram below, and using an acrylic ruler, template, and pencil, lightly mark the zigzagged shape on the top layer of canvas. Start by centering a 4" x 18" rectangle. Then, center 4 triangles, with their 4" bases in a row along long edges.

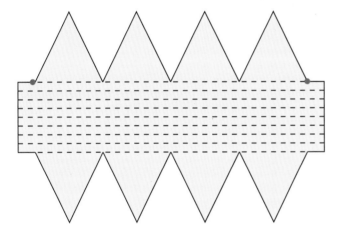

3 Pin canvas layers to prevent shifting, then scissors-cut along marked lines to make 2 zigzagged pieces.

4 Topstitch along the edges of the triangles on one edge of zigzagged piece. Since the top row of triangles will fold down to show the reverse side of the fabric, you must flip the piece over to topstitch the opposite edge with the heavier thread. For more decorative stitching, echo-quilt inside each triangle, following the b dash lines (stitching lines) in the actual-size pattern on page 19. Remember to turn the piece over to the reverse side to echo-stitch triangles on the opposite edge.

The Eco-Friendliest!

Organic cotton fabrics are grown without the use of environmentally harmful pesticides and herbicides. Undyed, unbleached, natural colored fabrics just may be the most eco-logical choice you can make.

5 Position one zigzagged piece so that the heavy thread is on the wrong side on top, and so the corners as indicated by green dots on the diagram (below, left) are 2" from top corners of opened tote. Pin in place. Stitch rows approximately ½" apart across canvas rectangle and through canvas tote, as indicated by short dash lines on diagram.

6 Repeat to add second zigzagged piece to other side of bag.

Topsy Curvy Bag

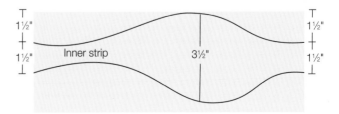

1 Trim doubled canvas fabric to 1" longer than width of canvas tote. Place double layer of canvas on a cutting mat. Using a rotary cutter but no ruler, cut gently curving lines. If you aren't comfortable doing this freehand, lightly pencil a guideline to follow. For the inner strip, begin and end 1½" from top corners and curve gradually up to the top edge in the middle. Rotary-cut a second gently curving line, starting and ending 3" from top corners, and descending in the middle so that widest part of finished strip is 3½".

2 Center one inner strip on top of remaining doubled canvas. Rotary-cut a wider, randomly curvy strip that extends ½" to 2" beyond the inner strip; see the outer strip on the diagram below.

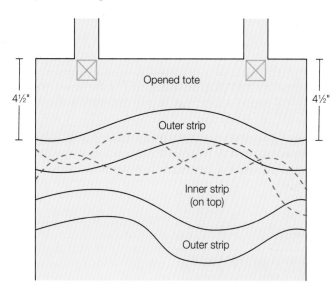

Opened tote

4½"

4½"

Outer strip

Inner strip
(on top)

Outer strip

3 Center one inner strip on an outer strip and pin both to the opened tote bag, with the ends 4½" from the top corners. Repeat at the other end of the opened tote. Using the same 4½" measurement will allow some curves to line up when bag is reassembled.

4 Topstitch approximately ¼" from raw edges of inner and outer strips. Also stitch additional swooping curves that move across inner and outer strip, as shown by short dash lines on the diagram.

Double the texture

Rotary-cut another set of overlapping, curvy strips, and topstitch them below the first set. If your bag has a logo printed or sewn on it, this is a great way to cover it up! (See page 50 for more ways to lose the logo.)

Do-it-yourself design

Try concentric circles, or rounds of flower petals and a flower center, or hexagons. Alternatively, use layers of the same size, and get a real chenille effect.

Squares in Squares Bag

1 Fold canvas fabric crosswise in half and pin at intervals to keep layers from shifting.

2 Lay acrylic rulers on the bias of the canvas and cut the following pairs: three 4" squares, three 2½" squares, and three 1" squares. Note: If you have a 4" and a 2½" square acrylic ruler, you can make quick work of rotary cutting the big and medium-size squares.

3 Center one 4" square on opened tote, 2½" from top edge. Position another 4" square to either side, ½" apart. Pin, then topstitch close to edges.

4 Pin one 2½" square centered on each 4" square and topstitch in place. Pin one 1" square centered on each 2½" square, and topstitch in place. Repeat to add 3 concentric squares to other side of tote. 🍂

Sew
SIMPLE

*Mix & match your way to a unique look!
These tote-ally terrific designs offer exciting
inspirations for your own easy-to-sew bags.*

Say Aloha

by Virginia Avery

TO GET PRAISE FOR YOUR QUILT, Virginia Avery reasoned in her 1982 book, <u>Quilts to Wear</u>, you have to invite friends over, clean your house, and serve refreshments. No such bother, she explained, with wearables: "You simply wear your handiwork and go wherever the action is. What you wear proclaims your talent more boldly than a billboard." Jinny routinely extended this philosophy to her bags. The high-contrast design here was an attention-grabbing signpost for her Hawaiian appliqué workshop, and held all her class samples. Try this Polynesian art form and turn unique, paper-folded patterns into stunning needlework. Or, let another quilting technique emblazon this classic tote. In any case, your bag will say, "Aloha! Check out the high style over here!"

What you'll need

Dimensions: 17" x 17" x 3½" deep

- Pre-washed, pre-shrunk fabric:
  1 yard of solid red or bright color of your choice
  1 yard of white (here, a bleached muslin)
  1 yard of lining (here, a red print), plus ⅜ yard more for each inner pocket

- 100% cotton batting (Jinny used Fairfield's Cotton Classic; see Resources, page 61), 20" x 54"

- 1 yard of fusible interfacing

- Freezer paper

- Paper-cutting scissors and small, sharp scissors

Cutting

From red fabric, cut:
  Two 18" squares
  Two 4" x 26" strips, for handles
  Two 4½" x 18" strips

From white fabric, cut:
  Two 22" squares
  Two 18" squares

From lining fabric, cut:
  Two 18" squares
  One or two 13" x 30" rectangle(s), for pocket(s)
  Three 4½" x 18" rectangles

From batting, cut:
  Two 22" squares
  Three 4½" x 18" rectangles, for gusset
  Two 1¾" x 24" strips

From fusible interfacing, cut:
  Two 13" squares, for pockets

Hawaiian appliqué

1 Cut freezer paper into a 14" square. Fold in half horizontally, waxy side in. Fold in half vertically, to form a square, then fold diagonally, into eighths. Staple through

the layers in two or three places to keep them from shifting. Working freehand, cut out shapes along the folded and cut edges. Organic shapes, such as stalks, leaves, flowers, pods, and fruit are often used in Hawaiian appliqué. Keep in mind that teardrops, hearts, circles, ovals, and other gentle curves will be the easiest to appliqué. After cutting, gently remove the staples and unfold. Assess your design, and consider refolding, re-stapling, and cutting more shapes or enlarging one or two you have.

2 When you are satisfied with your pattern, iron it, with the freezer paper's waxy side down, centered on one 18" red square.

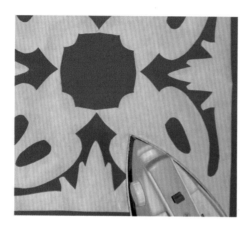

3 Using a soft lead or fabric pencil in a color that shows up well, lightly trace along the edges of the paper cut-out. Take a small snip in the center of each open shape.

4 Remove the freezer paper and lay the red piece on an 18" white square. Pin, then baste in unsnipped areas, keeping ¼" away from any openings.

5 Work from the center outward as follows, but only on one opening at a time. Insert the tip of a small, sharp scissors into a snipped area, and cut to within ¼" along a straight edge or very gentle curve, and within a few threads at inside corners.

For needle-turn reverse appliqué, use red thread, or color to match the top layer, and knot the thread end. Bring the needle up through the back of the white fabric alongside a cut-out. Use the length of the needle to gently turn under the edges. Hold this edge down with the thumbnail of one hand, while you take tiny slipstitches to almost invisibly secure the edges of the red cut-out to the white background. After completing one cut-out, fasten off on the back (white side, behind red fabric), or travel over to the next opening, reinforce thread with a backstitch, and continue.

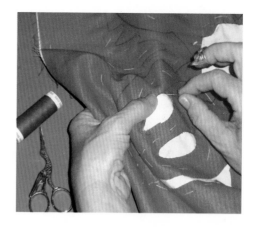

6 Continue until all interior cut-outs have been appliquéd. Proceed to cut through the red fabric along the freezer paper's outer edge, if desired, and appliqué to expose the white fabric for ¼" to ½".

7 If desired, repeat steps 1 through 6 to work reverse appliqué on a second set of red and white squares, using the same or a different freezer paper pattern for other side of bag.

Beyond Hawaii

Let your bag sport any design. Adopt an orphan (left-over quilt block) to feature on the front, or put a UFO (UnFinished Object of your labors) to good use. Quilt a plain block for the back.

Quilting

1 Make a quilt sandwich by centering one reverse appliqué square on 22" squares of batting and white fabric. Baste the layers together. Hand-quilt, using red thread on red fabric and white thread on white fabric. Start from the center of the design and echo-quilt, following the contours of each shape, and spacing lines of quilting evenly.

2 When quilting is complete, square up each piece, with the design centered.

Outer bag

1 For the gusset, center each red 4½" wide strip on a same-size piece of batting. Baste layers and stitch them together end to end.

Virginia Avery

Port Chester, New York

Since the 1970s, Virginia Avery has been known for her sweeping entrances at major quilting shows and events, outfitted in one of her dramatic quilted jackets, with matching hat and bag. Totally self-taught in clothing construction, Jinny made her first dress at age 12, not realizing one was supposed to use a pattern. As an accomplished jazz pianist who played with the King Street Stompers for more than fifty years, Jinny has always been tuned in to the art of improvisation. She has conveyed her ideas and inspired the quilt world as a teacher and author of books on appliqué and wearables. The very first artist recruited to submit wearable art for The Fairfield Fashion Show at Quilt Market, she is a Silver Star and Quilters Hall of Fame honoree.

2 With right sides together, pin the long edges of the joined gusset around the completed bag front, matching gusset seams to bottom corners of the bag front. Using a walking foot (or more pins to keep layers from shifting) and a longer stitch, join these pieces together, ½" from raw edges and pivoting at the corners. In the same way, join the opposite edge of the gusset to the second square.

Lining

1 If desired, add inside pockets: For each, position a 13" square of interfacing, fusible side down, at one end of 13" x 30" lining piece on the wrong side. Press to fuse. Fold lining crosswise in half, right side in, and stitch around, ¼" from the edges, leaving the edge without interfacing open. Clip corners, turn pocket to the right side, and press. Hem top edge: fold open edges ¼" to the inside, then 1¾" to wrong side over interfacing; stitch in place. Center pocket on an 18" square of lining fabric. Stitch around all but hemmed edge.

2 Assemble the lining similarly to the bag: First join the three 4½" x 32" lining strips end to end for the lining gusset. Join them to one 18" lining square, then to the other, but leave open for 8" along one side.

Assembly

1 For each handle, baste a 1¾" x 26" strip of batting to wrong side of a 4" x 26" red strip, ¼" from one long edge. Fold red strip lengthwise in half, with right side in, and stitch ¼" from raw edges to form a tube. Turn to right side; press flat with seam along one long edge. Topstitch ¼" from both long edges. Pin ends of one handle to bag front, 3½" from the center. Repeat with bag back.

2 Place lining over the bag, with right sides together. Pin, matching seams and ensuring that handles are in between the layers. Stitch all around top edge, ½" from raw edges.

3 Pull bag to right side through opening in side of lining. Turn open edges to inside, and whipstitch opening closed. Stitch into bag along gusset, ½" from seam, through all layers, and as far as machine needle can reach.

Virginia Avery used another version of her paper-fold design to adorn the other side of the bag. You may prefer to do a simple, quilted wholecloth design instead, using the same snowflake pattern but no cutwork or appliqué stitching.

Fine Feathered Bag

by Diane Gaudynski

"FEATHERS ARE MY FAVORITE THING to quilt," says Diane Gaudynski, *"and I like to let them form as I work, with no plan ahead of time."* In her machine quilting classes, even beginners find themselves admiring feathers and other beautiful samples they've created. Diane suggests that, instead of sticking such classy class work in a closet, students combine two practice squares, add a quilted gusset, bind the raw edges, and go show off. Such a fashion statement guarantees you'll look très chic, whether you're shopping in jeans and a T-shirt, or carrying homemade goodies to the fanciest party. Either way, there couldn't be a prettier feather in your cap!

What you'll need

Dimensions: 16" x 16" x 6" deep

- Fabric:
  1½ yards for bag exterior and binding; here, Diane used a blue hand-dyed cotton
  ⅔ yard for bag interior (which can become the bag exterior, as the bag is reversible!); here, Diane used a delicate blue and cream floral print

- Batting, 18" x 60" (Diane recommends wool)

- #100 silk thread (YLI; see Resources, page 61), a shade darker than the fabric, for the feather design, and a lighter blue for the background

- Pair of satin cord drapery tie-backs, 27"

- Four 1" mother-of-pearl buttons

Cutting

From fabric for bag exterior, cut:
Two 16½" squares

5½" x 50" rectangle; cut along the lengthwise grain (parallel to the selvages), and pieced as necessary for length
2½"-wide strips on the bias, totaling 150" in combined length, for binding

From fabric for interior cut:
Two 18" squares
7" x 52" rectangle, cut along the lengthwise grain, and pieced as necessary for length

From batting, cut:
Two 18" squares
7" x 52" rectangle, pieced as necessary for length

Machine quilting

1 While this machine quilting design is done freehand, you'll want to lightly mark guidelines for the central spines of your feather designs. Work directly on one 16½" square. To follow Diane's design, first fold fabric into quarters, and crease the folds, then open. Tape it to a work surface to keep it taut, and lightly pencil or use quilter's chalk.

Don't ruffle your feathers

Not confident enough to machine-quilt freehand? No problem: use a purchased stencil and trace inside the openings, or use a light box or sunny window to trace a continuous line pattern.

2 Refer to diagrams (a, b, and c), in which the long dash lines represent the creases, and draw curves, positioning them in the corresponding quarters. Start by drawing the center two large curves as shown in purple on diagram a. Beginners may want to just work with those guidelines as the spines for two graceful plumes! For a more complex design, mark a few curvy offshoots as shown in green on diagram b. Diane's design has even more offshoots that you might like to try if you are an advanced quilter; see the turquoise lines on diagram c.

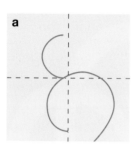

a

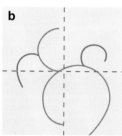

b

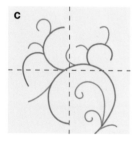

c

3 Make a quilt sandwich for the front, back, and gusset: place interior fabric right side down on a flat surface, position same-size pieces of batting on top, and center corresponding exterior pieces, right side up. Baste, using safety pins in the time-honored way. Or, baste by hand or machine—but only with water-soluble thread. (A spritz of water or quick dunk and air-dry will remove the markings and the thread afterwards.)

4 Before you free-motion quilt, check out Diane G's Top 5 Tips on the right. Use a darning foot and let the simple markings guide your quilting. Begin at the base of any feather. (See the red dot on the detail photo.) Pull bobbin thread up and make 3 stitches in one place, then clip thread ends. Quilt down one side of the feather to the tip, making graceful, teardrop shapes that gradually increase, then decrease in size (see red dash lines). Then, turn around (see black dot and short, black dash lines) and quilt around the outside of the feather back to the starting

DIANE G'S TOP 5 TIPS FOR FREE-MOTION QUILTING

1. Pick a thread color that blends with your fabric. Use the same color thread but a lighter weight in the bobbin.

2. Keep a sample of the exact same top, batt, and backing at your machine, so you can practice before you tackle the real project and warm up before every sitting.

3. To get a perfect, balanced stitch on the top and back, adjust top tension, lowering the number by one until stitches curve gently and meet the bottom thread in the batting.

4. Keep stitch length even and appropriate for your thread choice and your skill level. Diane uses #100 YLI silk, a fine cotton in the bobbin, a 1.6 mm stitch length, and echo-quilting lines of stippling only 1/16" apart. Less advanced and less ambitious quilters might be happy with a heavier thread, longer stitches and minimal echo-quilting in background areas.

5. Run the machine at medium speed and keep hand movements even. To push the quilt sandwich around smoothly, try a Free Motion Slider (See Resources) on the bed of your machine. Better than wearing gloves!

point, closely echoing contours of teardrops. Next, machine-quilt teardrop shapes down the other side of the feather to the tip, and work a line of echo quilting back

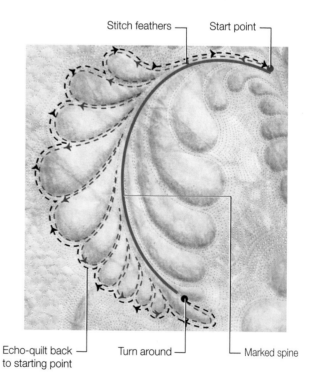

Stitch feathers — Start point

Echo-quilt back to starting point — Turn around — Marked spine

Diane Gaudynski

Waukesha, Wisconsin
www.dianegaudynski.net

I've heard expert quilters whisper, "I'd forget all about hand-quilting if I could machine-quilt like Diane Gaudynski." Yes indeedy, Diane has won numerous awards at major quilt competitions and her quilts have been exhibited internationally, in galleries and museums as well as private collections. She has six quilts in the permanent collection of the National Quilt Museum and one at the International Quilt Study Center. She lectures and teaches nationally. To learn more about Diane's techniques, including how to achieve the echo quilting, clamshell texture, and *"Diane-shiko"* pattern on the gussets of the bag, check out her book, *Quilt Savvy: Gaudynski's Guide to Machine Quilting* (AQS).

up. At the end of a feather or section, make 3 stitches in one place and clip thread ends.

5 Repeat step 4 for each curve and offshoot of the design. Then, if desired, fill in the background with rows or rounds of echo quilting, following the contours of each feather.

6 For the gusset, use a walking foot and quilt a simple, allover design.

Assembly

1 When front, back, and gusset are all quilted, spray the pieces with water to remove any marking residue, or gently wash in lukewarm water and let air-dry flat. On each piece, trim backing and batting even with quilt top and square them up, making sure that squares are identical in size. Use pins to mark the center of the gusset and the bottom of the front and back squares.

2 With wrong sides facing, pin gusset to bag front; first match the centers, then pin the corners and side edges. Using cotton thread, a walking foot, a scant ¼" seam, and a longer stitch, join these pieces; pivot carefully at each corner. Trim off the overhang of the gusset so it's even with the top edges of bag front.

3 Join 2½" bias strips to make binding 8" longer than will go around the two sides and bottom of bag. Fold strip lengthwise in half and press, stretching binding a bit as you move the iron. Pin binding to gusset, starting

from opening of bag and keeping raw edges even. With a walking foot, stitch along binding through all layers, ¼" from edges. Pivot at corners and take several small stitches there to secure. Fold binding over to bag front and pin. Working from gusset side, stitch in the ditch (sew over the seam) along binding, catching the binding edge on bag front. Trim away excess binding strip.

4 In the same way, stitch gusset to bag back, and add binding. Then, starting at the center of one gusset end, bind top edge of bag.

5 To secure handles, stitch a button to the top edge of bag on front and back, 4½" from the gusset. Slip loops of a drapery tie-back over each button on the front. Repeat on the back with a second tie-back.

The secret to plumes that pop!

Shhh, don't tell, just do like Diane: Shade edges of each puffy teardrop with artist's pencil a little darker than your fabric and highlight centers with a brush of ink in a lighter color. Heat-set.

14-Carrot Gold

by Eleanor Levie

I ADMIT IT, I can't resist a groaner of a pun . . . I'll even stoop to creating a quilt or quilted design around one, as with this fresh, fun tote. A Four-Patch of yellow-gold prints lays out a garden bed for seven carrots on each side. The bag's interior and wrap-around gusset include pockets and gold-toned hardware for closing the bag or hooking your keys. So as a carryall, the bag is as good as gold for holding your car keys, coupons and cash, as well as lots of treasures from the market.

What you'll need

Dimensions: 18" x 14½" x 6" deep

- Fabric:
  4 different yellow-gold prints, for background—2 fat
    eighths of each, or 10" x 15" pieces
  3" x 9" rectangles of 7 different orange prints, for carrots
  ½ yard gold plaid fabric, for lining and inside pocket
  ⅜ yard light green print, for gusset exterior
  ½ yard green dot print, for binding

- ¾ yard of lightweight paper-backed fusible web, 17" wide

- Timtex,* 22" wide, 1 yard

- Thin batting, 14" x 45" (Nature-fil Bamboo Batting* by
  Fairfield Processing Corp. was used here)

- Orange, yellow and green sewing or machine quilting
  thread

- Green satin cord, 2 yards each green in ¼" and ⅛"
  thickness, and 2 yards of lime green*

- 1¼ yards of yellow plastic webbing,* 1" wide

- 1 package of gold-toned hook fasteners*

- 1 gold-toned D-ring*

- Basting spray

*See Resources on page 61

Cutting

From each of the 4 fabrics for bag exterior, cut:
   Two 7½" x 9½" rectangles, for patches

From Timtex, cut two rectangles, 19" x 15".

From lining fabric, cut two 19" x 15" rectangles and one
7" x 52" strip, piecing as necessary

From light green print, cut two 6"-wide strips selvage to
selvage. From one of the strips, cut a 6" x 9" rectangle,
for pocket

From green dot fabric, cut 2½"-wide strips on the bias,
totaling 150" in combined length, for binding

From batting, cut a 7" x 52" rectangle, piecing butted
edges with whipstitching as necessary

From webbing, cut:
   Two 26" strips, for handles
   Four 4" strips, for hardware loops

Background

1 Arrange a Four-Patch block using one of each of the
four gold prints. Stitch top and bottom rectangles together
in pairs; press seam allowances in opposite directions.
Stitch the two rows together, nesting the seams and
pinning at the ends. Press seam allowances downward.

2 Repeat to make a Four-Patch block for the other side of the bag.

3 In a well-ventilated area, apply spray-baste to the wrong sides of Four-Patch blocks. Center each block on a Timtex rectangle and press to smooth and secure the bond, using a press cloth.

4 Mark a point 3" from each bottom corner. Place a ruler from this point to the top corner; cut through all layers. Trim other edges even with Four-Patch block. Edges should measure 18½" across the top, 12½" across the bottom; the height through the center should be 14½".

Carrots

1 Press fusible web to one side of remaining batting, and place that, paper side down, on an ironing surface.

2 Press fusible web to the back of each orange print rectangle, then remove the paper backing and position the pieces on the batting.

3 Using the actual-size carrot pattern shown here, trace, photocopy, or draw the shape onto cardstock and cut out to make a template. Place template on each fabric, and trace in pencil. Flip pattern around and trace a second carrot on each orange print, making slight variations in the sizes and shapes.

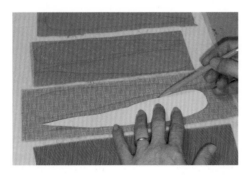

4 Cut out carrots, and arrange 7 on each main bag piece. Fuse in place. Using orange thread, blanket-stitch around each carrot. Begin near the top, and as you approach the tip, shorten the width of the stitch. Switch to a straight stitch and sew a long, string-like tip before blanket-stitching the opposite side. End near the top.

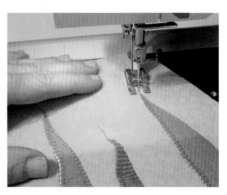

5 For the carrots' green stems, cut satin cord into 1" strands, and insert 5 to 7 strands at the top of each carrot. Using green thread and a darning foot, free-motion-stitch curved lines across the top of the carrot, securing the ends of the satin cord strands.

Lining

1 Use the bag front and back as patterns to cut three same-size pieces from lining fabric. For an inside pocket, cut one piece 1" smaller all around and stitch a generous hem along the long, top edge. Turn the side edges ½" to the wrong side and center on the right side of one full-size piece, with the bottom edges even. Pin, then stitch along the sides, ⅛" and ¼" from the edges.

2 Apply fusible web to the wrong side of lining pieces, remove paper backing, and press to Timtex side of bag front and back.

Gusset

1 Piece the 7"-wide strips of light green print to make a 7" x 52" strip. Make a quilt sandwich with 7" x 52" pieces of lining fabric, batting, and light green print. Use spray basting or pins to secure the layers temporarily, then quilt a few lines to secure them permanently.

2 Add a side pocket (see title page): On one 6" edge of the 6" x 9" rectangle of light green print, fold ¼", then 1" to wrong side and topstitch to hem the top of the pocket. Position the pocket by wrapping gusset around bag front. Center the pocket on one side of gusset. Turn the bottom edge of the pocket under, and pin. Fold pocket down and stitch across, through all layers. Then press pocket up again, and pin in place.

Assembly

1 With wrong sides facing, pin gusset to bag front; first matching the centers, then pinning the corners and side edges. Using a few pins, a longer stitch, and sewing a scant ¼" from edges, join these pieces, pivoting carefully at each corner. Don't trim the gusset ends even with the top edges of the bag just yet.

2 Join 2½" bias strips to make binding more than long enough to encase the two sides and bottom of bag. Fold strip lengthwise in half and press, stretching the binding a bit as you move the iron. Pin the binding to the bag front, starting from the top edge of the bag and keeping raw edges even. Stitch binding through all layers, ¼" from edges so that you cover the previous line of stitching. Stop stitching ¼" from the bottom corner, fold the binding up at an angle and then down, even with the bottom edge. Resume stitching ¼" from the corner. In the same way, miter the binding at the other corner.

3 Fold the binding over to the gusset and pin, then hand-baste in place. Working from the front of the bag, stitch in the ditch along the binding. Your stitches should catch the binding edge on the gusset. Trim away the excess binding strip. In the same way, stitch the gusset to the bag back, and add binding.

Show your bag who's boss

Completing the bag construction may be a bit challenging, as the Timtex-covered pieces can be cumbersome. Just flex, roll, and push them into place or out of your way as needed.

4 Pin ends of webbing handles inside bag along top edge, 4" from the center. Slip each of three 4" strands through the loop of a gold hook fastener, and fourth one through a D ring. Bring raw ends together, and pin one to each top of the gusset, on outside of bag. Pin the third to center of bag front, on inside. Pin ends with D ring to center of bag back, also inside.

5 Starting at the center of one gusset end, bind the top edge of the bag, as described in steps 2 and 3 at left. Fold each handle end 1½" below the top rim, and following the Bag Basics on page 63, stitch a boxed criss-cross to reinforce. Do the same for each hardware loop.

Grow baby carrots

Why not plant a carrot on matching accessories—an eyeglasses case, a cell phone pouch, a cover for pocket-size facial tissues, or a cosmetics bag?

A Tisket, A Tasket

by Jane Sassaman

"IN EUROPE, IT'S FASHIONABLE to personalize your bike, as it is everyone's main mode of travel," reflected Jane Sassaman after teaching on a recent quilting cruise. So, when challenged to design a shopping bag for this book, she kept fuel-free transport like biking, hiking, and walking top of mind. The outcome was a clever basket liner with a roomy drawstring dome, perfect for a bike or a small sturdy carryall. Just the thing for light shopping or dashing off on a picnic! Jane used her own nature-inspired fabrics for this unique tote. Felt balls dangle at the ends of ties that ensure nothing falls out. Who says organic style can't be fun and funky?

What you'll need

Dimensions: 13" x 7" x 8" high (plus dome)

- Bike basket or Lace Shopping Basket* (see photo on page 38); for other sized baskets, adjust all fabric amounts and measurements as needed

- Preshrunk fabrics:
  1¼ yards of black hot pink print* for liner and ties, plus another ¼ yard, for interior pockets
  ⅜ yard of black print for dome
  ¾ yard of heavy-weight interfacing/stabilizer such as Timtex,* 22" wide

- Handmade felt ball beads*: Package of 18 2.5cm handmade felt beads—Cool (assorted blue and green shades); package of 18 1cm felt mini beads —multicolored

- 18 square beads, 6mm, in coordinated colors

*See Resources on page 61

Sized for your basket

1 Take measurements of the inside of the basket you will use: the width and length of the bottom, the height of the sides, and if the sides are angled, the length of the rim along the long edge and along the short edge. Replace

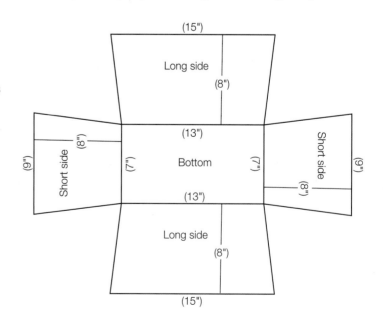

Jane Sassaman

Harvard, Illinois
www.janesassaman.com

Jane Sassaman is a contemporary quilt artist, known for bold exuberant designs, drenched in color and celebrating the energy of the garden. She was juried into Quilt National six times, and judged the prestigious art forum in 2001. Her quilt, "Willow," was named one of "America's 100 Best Quilts of the 20th Century." Jane designs fabric for FreeSpirit, and credits Arts & Craft icon William Morris, the Finnish design company Marimekko, and textile artist Kaffe Fassett as inspirations for her designing. In workshops, Jane endows participants with creative confidence. The Sassaman Store, on her website, carries her patterns, publications, and more.

the measurements in parentheses on the diagram (page 36) with those for your basket.

2 For each panel of liner—bottom, long sides, and short sides—cut two rectangles from liner fabric 1" larger than measurements you recorded, to include ½" seam allowances. Also for each panel, cut one rectangle from Timtex, ¼" smaller than the recorded measurements.

In the mood for motley?

Since all the panels of the liner are cut separately, there's nothing to prevent you from making each one with a different fabric, or with patchwork.

Liner assembly

1 Work with one set of panels at a time. With wrong sides together, sew ends of short and long side panels to adjacent edges of bottom panel, as shown on diagram (page 36), leaving ½" seam allowances and starting and stopping ½" from corners. Press seam allowances toward the side panels.

2 With right sides together, sew the edges of the side panels together, beginning at the bottom corners and working upward, making ½" seams. Press these seam allowances open.

Extra! Extra! Special addition!

After step 1, while panels are still flat: This is the time to stitch pockets for a cell phone, iPod, or Blackberry, and "girdles" to hold bottles upright. Check out the how-to's on page 39.

3 Repeat steps 1 and 2 to assemble the second set of panels. Place the two pieced liners together with wrong sides facing. Insert the piece of Timtex for the bottom between the layers. Sew over the seams (stitch in the ditch) around the bottom, encasing the Timtex.

4 Match side seams and pin, then stitch in the ditch along the seams. You will be creating 4 "pockets." Slip a corresponding piece of Timtex into each pocket. Baste along the top of the liner, ½" from the top.

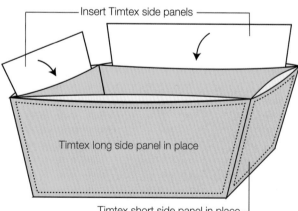

Insert Timtex side panels

Timtex long side panel in place

Timtex short side panel in place

Ties and drawstring dome

1 For ties, cut 16 strips, 1½" x 13", from basket liner fabric. Fold each lengthwise in half, over a l5" strand of string or yarn, with right side inside. Sew across one end and long side ¼" from edges; avoid stitching over strand. Pull the strand from the open end to turn tie to the right side; remove string and press.

2 Test-fit liner in basket and pin 4 ties along each side, at logical places for securing liner to your basket, Baste the ties to the top edge of the outer layer, with raw edges even.

3 Measure around top edge of liner and divide measurement in half. For dome lining, cut two rectangles from the same fabric as liner to this length plus 1", each with a width equal to height of basket plus 1". For dome, cut two same-size rectangles from contrasting fabric.

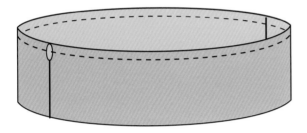

4 Join matching dome liner rectangles along short sides to form a loop. Do the same thing on the contrast dome rectangles, but begin the seam ⅞" from the top corner on one side, leaving an opening for the drawstring. Press seam allowances open, including the ⅞" opening.

5 Place contrast fabric dome and dome lining pieces right sides together with seams aligned. Stitch along top edge. Turn right side out, and press. Stitch ⅝" from folded edge, to form a drawstring casing.

6 Pin right side of contrast fabric dome to top edges of liner, positioning the drawstring opening at the center of basket liner's short side. Stitch ½" from edges, taking care not to catch lining in the seam. Turn raw edge of lining ½" to the wrong side, and pin this folded edge in place around the inside of the basket liner, so it encases the raw edges of basket liner and contrast fabric dome. Topstitch along this edge, through all layers.

7 Make a long drawstring, using a 1½" x 50" strip of contrast dome fabric and referring to step 1 for ties. Use a safety pin to guide drawstring through drawstring casing.

CRADLE YOUR BREAKABLES

Pockets for a cell phone, iPod, or Blackberry
From tote lining fabric, cut two rectangles, 1¼" wider than electronic item, and ½" shorter. Place rectangles together, right sides facing, and stitch around, leaving 2" on one short side open. Clip corners, turn to right side through the opening, and press. Also press open edge ¼" to the inside. Topstitch along one long edge, which will be the top edge. If desired, stitch over elastic trim pulled taut, so pocket will hug the item. Make a ⅜" pleat, ½" from each bottom corner; pin. Position pocket on the loose,

inside/lining piece of tote, close to the bottom. Topstitch along sides and bottom edge. After tote is assembled, reinforce the stitching at the top corners of pocket, sewing through all layers.

Bottle girdle
From the tote lining fabric, cut a 9½" x 11½" rectangle. Fold lengthwise in half, right sides together. Stitch along all but one short side, ¼" from the edges. Clip corners, turn to right side through the open end, and press, turning open edges ¼" to the inside as well. If desired, stitch over elastic trim pulled taut, so girdle will hug the bottle. Tape the center of the bottle girdle to a sample bottle, 1" from the bottom, and place bottle in your bag or lining. Tape ends of bottle girdle to sides of tote lining, to properly secure the bottle, then remove the bottle and pin. Topstitch along ends, through the lining. After tote is assembled, stitch ½" to the inside of these topstitches, through all layers of the tote.

8 Embellish ends of ties and drawstring: use an X-Acto knife to slit a larger opening in each 2.5cm felt ball bead. Use tweezers or a seam ripper to push one end of tie into slit. Thread a long needle with doubled sewing thread or beading thread, and tie a knot. Insert needle through the end of the tie embedded in felt ball bead, and out the opposite hole. Continue through holes of a contrast color 1cm felt ball bead, and a glass bead. Guide the thread around the glass bead, back through the felt beads. Repeat, and then fasten off.

Pocket Masterpiece

by Lonni Rossi

WHY NOT DISPLAY A MINI QUILT in an unexpected, but delightful place—on the big, outer pocket of a tote bag? Lonni Rossi shares her simple and simply divine secrets for creating a little gem in fabric and thread. Take inspiration with this surprisingly sophisticated composition appliquéd with fabrics from Lonni's quilter's cotton collections, and you might just go on to become a confident art quilter like Lonni! (Of course, there's no reason traditional quilters couldn't adorn the pocket of a tote bag with a classic mini.) Set off your mini-masterpiece with heavy-weight hemp. "It's luscious in this vibrant poppy-red," raves Lonni. "It's crisp, it softens more every time it's washed and it's a faster-growing, more sustainable fiber than cotton." Whether you're into art, craft, or the environment (or all three!), this could be your bag.

What you'll need for this bag

Dimensions: 17½" x 15" x 7" deep

- Fabrics:
  1 yard of hemp* in Poppy Red
  Small amounts (fat eighths or less) of various prints with quiet visual textures in various shades of green, plus contrasting prints in rust, sepia, ochre, and solid black (these are from Lonni's *Paintbox* and *Petals* collections for Andover*)

- Fusible web such as Pellon Wonder Under

- Iron-on, tear away stabilizer such as Sulky Totally Stable, 10" x 14"

- Batting (this is Nature-fil Bamboo Batting* from Fairfield Processing Corp.), 10" x 14"

- Rayon decorative threads (Lonni used Sulky 30 weight rayon,* solid, variegated and Ultra-Twist)

*See Resources on page 61

Cutting

From hemp fabric, cut along the grain:
  Two 43" x 20" rectangles for outer bag and lining
  Two 16½" x 13" rectangles for pocket
  Two 3" x 22" strips for handles

Making a mini-quilt

1 Refer to the schematic diagram on page 42 and actual-size leaf detail on page 43. Iron fusible web to the back of all print fabrics.

2 To create circle sections #2 and #4, use a compass and either a fabric-marking pencil or a fine-tip marker. Scribe circles on the right sides of fabrics backed with fusible web. Vary diameters from 1" to 4" in diameter, in ½" increments. Peel off release paper, then cut out the circles just to the inside of the marked line.

A hot tip for circling around

No compass or marking! Put fusible web-backed fabric folded into quarters on a cutting mat, position a Mini Cut A Round tool (see Resources) on top, and rotary-cut through the slots.

3 Start with the largest circles and fuse onto a 12" x 10" piece of release paper, parchment paper, or Teflon presser sheet. Fuse smaller circles, centered on top, and also in between circles, until the area is completely filled and no empty spaces remain. Using a rotary cutter and ruler, cut two rectangles from fused composition: one 3½" x 8⅞" for section #2; and a second, 3¾" x 8⅞", for section #4.

4 Fuse each rectangle to stabilizer and then cut the stabilizer ½" larger all around. Using a darning foot and contrast-color rayon thread, free-motion stitch around each ring of the circles.

5 For section #1: Cut a 2" x 8⅞" rectangle from both brown and black fabrics. Sew pieces together along one long edge, and press. Refer to the actual-size detail photo (page 43, top) and trace a half-leaf to make template. Cut 3 half-leaves from light green and 3 from dark green fabrics. Peel off paper backing and fuse onto brown/black rectangle as shown to complete section #1. Lay on section #2, right sides together, stitch a ¼" seam along long left edge, flip section #1 to the left, and press.

6 For section #3, cut an olive green rectangle, 3¼" x 8⅞". Using the half-leaf template, trace half-leaf shapes onto fabric with chalk pencil. This will be quilted later. Sew section #3 to the right edge of section #2.

7 For section #4, use the wider piece of the circles fabric, 3¾" x 8⅞" and sew to right edge of section #3. Your mini-quilt is almost complete. Trim to 12½" x 8¾".

8 Add decorative stitching to the mini quilt: First, apply iron-on stabilizer to the back. Add additional free-motion stitching around the circles and stitch veins on the leaves. Satin-stitch along the outer edges of largest circles.

Make the pocket

1 Place the 2 pocket rectangles together and stitch ½" from edges around all but 4" centered on one long side—this will be the bottom. Clip corners and turn to right side and steam-press, turning open edges ½" to the inside.

2 Back the mini quilt with batting trimmed slightly smaller all around. Center the mini quilt on the pocket, with open edge at the bottom. Pin in place, then stitch in the ditch between sections and around mini quilt to secure it in place. Echo-quilt around the leaves on Section #1.

3 Satin-stitch along the centers of the leaves, around the leaves, between sections, and all around the mini quilt.

Assembly

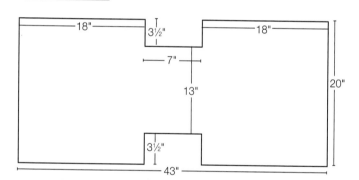

1 Referring to the diagram above and using a square or rectangular acrylic ruler and a fabric marking pencil in a contrast color, mark two 3½" squares from the middle of the long edges of the 43" x 20" hemp rectangles. Cut these squares away, to allow for a boxed bottom.

Not a burn mark!

Hemp changes color when you hit it with a hot steam iron, which is necessary for getting nice, flat edges. Don't be concerned, as the fabric will return to its original color as it cools.

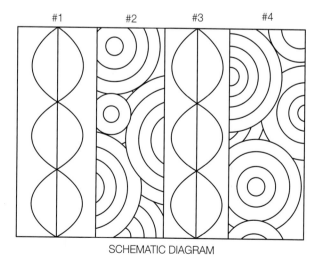

SCHEMATIC DIAGRAM

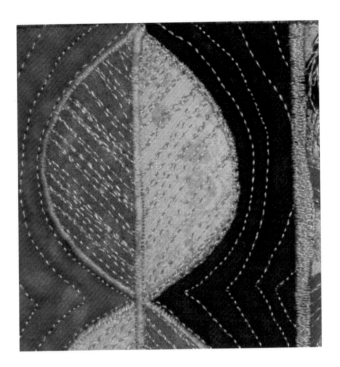

how-to's on page 20, pull, pin, and stitch the square cut-out to box the bottom. Repeat with the second shaped hemp piece, which serves as a lining. Steam-press outer bag and lining, and insert the lining inside the outer bag, with wrong sides facing and side seams aligned.

4 Stitch handles: Fold each 3" x 22" strip lengthwise in half, and steam-press. Unfold, then press both long raw edges ½" to the wrong side, and steam press. Refold lengthwise to form a 1" x 22" strip. Topstitch along the long edges.

5 Refold top edges to the inside. Insert ends of handles for 2" between the outer bag and lining, 5" from the center. Pin. Topstitch around top of bag, and secure handle ends with a boxed criss-cross; see page 63. Reinforce the pocket: following the previous lines of topstitching, stitch along the side edges of the pocket through all layers.

2 Center the pocket on one shaped piece, 5" from one 20" end, and centered between sides. Pin, then use matching thread to topstitch the sides and bottom, simultaneously closing the opening along pocket's bottom edge.

3 Turn the top edges on large, shaped hemp pieces 2" to wrong side, steam-press to crease, then unfold. Fold the large hemp piece with the pocket crosswise in half, so the pocket is on the inside. Stitch sides, ½" from edges. Press seam allowances open. Referring to Reconstruction

Did you know . . .

- **Renewable:** *In one growing season, hemp shoots up 15 to 25 feet, and bamboo, the fastest growing timber plant on earth, can soar 78 feet high.*
- **Organic:** *Neither hemp nor bamboo need much of any chemicals, pesticides, or fertilizers.*
- **Earth-friendly:** *Hemp breathes in more carbon dioxide than any other plant, and bamboo locks up all kinds of other greenhouse gases in its roots.*

Lonni Rossi

Ardmore, Pennsylvania
www.lonnirossi.com

An award-winning fiber artist and fabric designer, Lonni Rossi brings her sophisticated style to quilts, wearables, and luxurious home accessories. A former graphic designer, she incorporates fragmented text and evocative textures into her fabrics, whether they're her one-of-a-kind hand-painted and silk-screened works of art, or the commercial quilting cottons she designs for Andover Fabrics. Lonni also produces quilt patterns and kits and elegant commission work. She also teaches workshops on surface design. Somehow, she manages to fit in time to cuddle her new grand-daughter, too. Visit her at her retail shop and studio, Lonni Rossi Fabrics, 70 Rittenhouse Place, Ardmore, PA 19003, or online.

Seminole Inspiration

by Rachel D.K. Clark

IMPRESSED BY THE TRADITIONAL STITCHERY of Native Americans from the Florida Everglades region, wearable artist Rachel Clark loves to showcase Seminole-style patchwork. While the origins of the Seminole people go back 12,000 years and pieced designs were developed by Seminole women nearly a century ago, Rachel updates her version by combining a jelly roll of suede-look cotton in lots of different colors with rotary cutting and speed piecing. "I really enjoy these fast piecing techniques," she says. "The result looks labor-intensive and expensive, but it's <u>not</u>." Two rings of stuffed tubes make for comfy shoulder straps or double up for short tote bag handles, a design feature so versatile you'll want to apply it to any bag you make.

What you'll need

Dimensions: 25" x 15" x 6" deep

- Hand-dyed, suede look cotton fabrics from Cherrywood*:
  1 Cherry Roll (jelly roll), in Hot & Spicy or one 2½" x 44" wide strip of 24 assorted fabrics
  1 yard of Redwood (hereafter called brown) for main fabric

- ¾ yard of pre-shrunk muslin for foundation-piecing

- ¾ yard of desired fabric for lining

- 2 yards of cotton cording, ½" in diameter, for handles

- Fabric tube turning tool*

*See Resources on page 61

Rolling Logs (center band)

1 From brown fabric, cut four 1" strips across entire width of fabric. Cross-cut these into 18 strips, each 7" in length.

2 From Cherry Roll, cut 10 strips from assorted colors, each 4½" in length.

3 Also from brown fabric, cut 2 strips 1¾" x 27½"; cross-cut these into 20 rectangles, 1¾" x 2¾". Stitch one brown rectangle to each side of a colored strip, matching the 2½" edges; press. See diagram a. Repeat for each of the 4½" colored strips.

4 Rotary-cut each pieced strip lengthwise in half to form two 1⅜" x 7" strips. See diagram b. Place into two piles, one for front of bag, one for back.

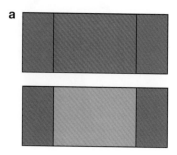

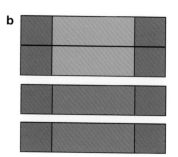

5 Referring to diagram c, arrange pieced strips from one pile in a row, alternating with 1"-wide brown strips, and with each subsequent colored bar staggered ¾" to the left. Aim roughly for a 60 degree-angle, with top corners of strips aligned along the sides. End with a pieced strip. Keeping the staggered arrangement, stitch strips together. Press. Using a ruler, cut a 5¼" x 12½" rectangle as shown. Repeat to make a Rolling Logs band for the back of bag.

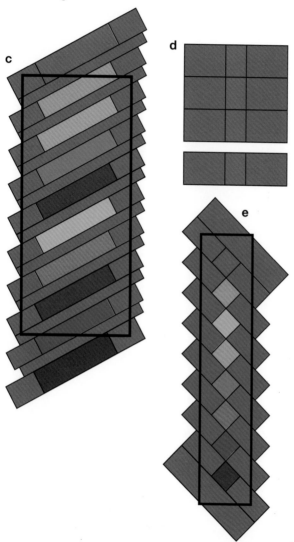

Shortcut to the finish line

Try any one of the Seminole patchwork techniques, and replace the others with a wide-striped fabric (a cheater strip set!) cut on the bias.

3 Place a brown strip on each side of a colored strip, matching the 6" edges. Pin and stitch; press. Cross-cut into 4 strips, each 1½" x 5"; see diagram d. Place each strip in a different pile. Repeat for each of the colored rectangles.

4 Referring to diagram e, stagger strips—each with a different color in the middle—by 1" to arrange a band. (You may wish to use same color order as for Rolling Logs.) Sew strips together, nesting seam allowances to match points of colored squares. Add a brown 1½" x 5" strip at the top and bottom. Press seam allowances downward.

5 Use an acrylic ruler to rotary-cut 1¼" to either side of vertical center of band, where points of colored squares line up. Also cut top and bottom edges, 6¼" from intersection of 4th and 5th squares. You will have a 2½" x 12½" rectangle. Repeat 3 times for 4 Diamond Rows.

SEMINOLE PATCHWORK

1. In this form of strip piecing, you'll join strips of different colors, slice them into narrow pieced strips, and combine the pieced strips in staggered arrangements.

2. Work on one type of patchwork at a time, making the bands for the front and back at the same time.

3. For all Seminole piecing, allow for 1/4" seam allowances and unless otherwise indicated, press seam allowances towards the main (brown) fabric.

4. Using a slightly mottled, hand-dyed fabric or a solid color that is the same on both sides means there is no right side vs. wrong side to worry about.

5. Perfect precision is not necessary! The word Seminole actually means wild, so don't feel you have to tame your piecing into absolute submission.

Diamond Row (squares on point)

1 From Cherry Roll, cut a 1½" x 6" rectangle from 8 different colors.

2 From brown fabric, cut 12 strips, 2¼" wide, selvage to selvage. Cross-cut strips into 6" lengths to get 72 rectangles, 2¼" x 6". Also cut 8 strips 1½" x 5".

Rachel D.K. Clark

Watsonville, California
www.rdkc.com

A long line of women going back at least as far as her great-grandmother give Rachel D.K. Clark a rich heritage in the sewing arts. Teacher, lecturer, and contemporary folk artist, Rachel routinely mixes traditional quiltmaking techniques with eclectic fabrics and vibrant designs. Since 1973, wearable art has been a major focus of her work, showcased in such venues as the Bernina Fashion Show, Threads magazine, and HGTV's Simply Quilts. Rachel's line of RDKC Patterns features classic jackets and coats that can incorporate panels of strip piecing and ethnic fabrics in high style.

Green Lightning (zigzag band)

1 Band #1: From brown, cut 2 strips 2½" x 18". From dark green, cut one strip 2½" x 18". Sew a brown strip to each side of dark green strip. Press towards the dark green strip. Cross-cut pieced unit into 28 strips, each 1¼" wide. See diagram f.

2 Band #2: From brown, cut two strips 2½" x 18". From sage green, cut one strip 1¼" x 18". Sew a brown strip to each side of sage green strip. Press towards the brown strips. Cross-cut pieced unit into 28 strips, each 1¼" wide. See diagram g.

3 Referring to diagram h, arrange 7 alternating bands #1 and #2 on an angle, so that sage and dark green fabrics are aligned. Sew bands together, nesting the seam allowances to match points. Press seam allowances downward.

4 Rotary-cut ¾" beyond the dark green corners on each side, so band is 3¼" wide. Square up the top and bottom, so band measures 12½" long. Repeat 3 times for 4 Green Lightning bands.

Side Bands

1 From leftover Cherry Roll strips in assorted colors, cut 36 strips ranging from 1" to 1½" wide and 10" long, piecing if necessary to get length.

2 Arrange 13 strips on the diagonal and cut other strips in half to create a rectangular arrangement; see diagram i. Sew strips together to create a pieced unit at least 8" x 12½". Cut unit into two rectangles, 3½" x 12½".

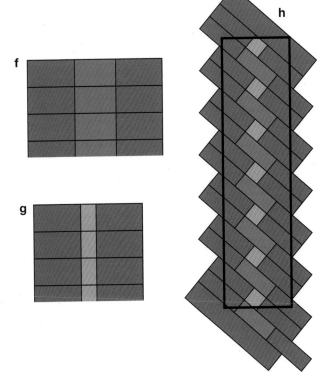

f

g

h

Quilt if desired!

The Seminoles didn't, and Rachel didn't, but you can quilt your patchwork. Layer batting over foundation. Then, as you add pieced sections with the flip-and-sew technique, you'll be quilting at the same time.

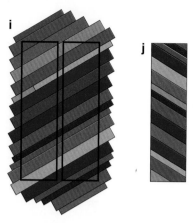

i

j

3 Follow step 2, but orient strips on the other diagonal (diagram j). Together, the two side bands will create a chevron effect.

Foundation-pieced assembly

1 Cut two 28" x 18" rectangles from muslin, for foundations.

2 Refer to diagram k throughout assembly. Fold one foundation crosswise in half. Fold a Rolling Logs band lengthwise in half. Matching the creases, position the band centered on the muslin, with top edges even. Pin. Repeat on second foundation.

3 Cut 4 accent strips, shown here in rust, 1" x 12½". Place one over each side of Rolling Logs band, with right sides together and edges even. Stitch, then flip outward, pressing and pinning in place. Working outward to one side, then the other, add Green Lightning band, a maroon accent strip (cut 4—1¼" x 12½"), a Diamond Row band, a purple accent strip (cut 4—1½" x 12½"), and a Side band. Repeat on the second foundation.

4 To form the bottom of the bag, cut 8 Cherry Roll strips, 1¼" x 20". Position one on the bottom edge, centered on the foundation-pieced area. Stitch and flip, then press. Add 3 more strips in the same way. Repeat on the second foundation.

5 Stay-stitch along edges of foundation-pieced sections. Trim away excess muslin, and trim sections if necessary to ensure they are the same size and shape.

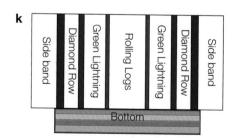

6 Use the resulting pieces as a template to cut 2 lining pieces. If desired, make pockets and stitch them to the lining.

7 Place foundation-pieced sections together, with right sides facing and bottom strips even. Stitch to join bottom strips, then press open. Fold in half along the striped bottom, with right sides together. Stitch together the long raw edges of the Side bands. Cut 2 accent strips, 1" x 12½". Fold long edges ¼" to wrong side; press. Cover each side seam with one accent strip; pin in place and then topstitch along the edges.

8 To give the bag a boxed bottom, pull the corners furthest from the side seam out taut. (See Bags Reborn on page 20.) Pin, and stitch across in a straight line, backstitching to reinforce the seam.

9 Create lining: Pin lining pieces together, stitch side seams, then box the bottoms same as for patchwork. Insert lining into outer bag, wrong sides together and side seams aligned.

Finishing

1 Add a wide binding to the rim of lined bag as follows: Cut fabric or join Cherry Roll strips together to get a 3¼"-wide strip long enough to go around the top of the bag (approximately 51"). Press this strip lengthwise in half, wrong side in. Beginning at a side seam, pin binding to bag, with raw edges even. Stitch ¾" from top edge. Flip binding over top edge to lining, fold raw edge under, pin, then slipstitch to secure. Tuck overlapping end of binding under neatly and slipstitch.

2 Make "belt loops" for handles to pass through: Cut 4 strips from brown fabric, 2" x 3¼". Fold long edges ½" toward the center, then fold lengthwise in half, encasing edges. Press. Tuck one short end in, then topstitch along edges. Stitch raw end to rim of binding inside bag, at top of Green Lightning band. Roll remainder of strip into a ring, with finished end even with slipstitched edge of binding. Repeat to make 4 loops.

3 For the handles, cut 2 strips, 2¼" x 36", from brown fabric. Fold each one lengthwise in half, right sides together, and sew along long edge, leaving ¼" seam allowances. Using the fabric tube turning tool with the ½" metal tube and following manufacturer's instructions, cover a 35½" strand of cotton cording. Pull through the loops on one side of the bag and butt ends together; whipstitch securely. Stitch three 1" x 2¼" rectangles of different-colored fabric together along their 2¼" sides; turn raw edges under, and wrap around the butted handle ends. Slipstitch in place. See photo, page 23.

Play with
PAINT

Whether you slap, dab, or drizzle, draw, doodle, airbrush, or squeegee, you'll discover a new frontier for quilters, and fun for kids of all ages. Get ready to tote your art!

Lose the Logo

by Eleanor Levie

IF YOU'RE LIKE ME, you've got a bunch of sturdy cloth tote bags lying around—maybe in your closet, or even in the trunk of your car! But they're all function, not form, and because of the brand names and commercial graphics printed on them, they're definitely not YOU! Remedy the situation with a little time, a bit of paint and your own brand of creativity—stamping, masking and brushing, marking, dripping or flicking paint. Too much fun to do alone, so arrange a play-date with a buddy of any age. After this quick and almost tote-al transformation, the only thing you'll be advertising is your fabulous style.

What you'll need

- Tote bag with a logo you'd like to hide

- Concentrated fabric paints for good coverage on dark fabric in assorted colors (here, Jacquard Neopaque starter set*)
- Acrylic craft paint
- Small paintbrushes, flat and tapered
- Round sponge applicators in various sizes (Spouncers* were used here)
- Permanent ink felt tip markers

- Duct tape
- Plastic cloth to protect tabletop surface, plastic gloves; plastic or aluminum pans or trays; plastic spoons and drink stirrers
- Optional: compressed sponges, corks, potato masher, pencil erasers

*See Resources on page 61

Color play

1 Protect work surface with an old shower curtain or plastic tablecloth. Insert cardboard into bag to keep paint from seeping through to the other side. Wear plastic gloves. Keep rags and paper towels handy for cleaning spills and drying brushes. Have jars of water available to keep brushes with paint on them from drying out.

2 Use disposable aluminum pie pans, foam meat trays, plastic egg cartons, margarine containers and lids for paint palettes. Mix paints with a drink stirrer or spoon. You can dip small paintbrushes into paint jars, but for stamping or mixing colors, spoon about a teaspoonful of paint onto palettes.

3 Keep brushes, sponges, and other paint applicators nearly dry when dipping them into paint. Apply thin coats of concentrated color to bags.

4 If your bag is vinyl or plastic-coated, let painted surfaces "cure" for 24 hours before using. Be gentle when spot-cleaning or washing your bag and do touch ups if paint flakes or wears off.

5 If your bag is cotton, linen, or polyester, heat-set the painted design, spreading a pressing cloth on top and applying a hot dry iron for a few seconds on each area.

Camouflage tactics

1 First, consider how to best cover up the logo and other printing on the bag. Use strips of duct tape to mask those areas you do not want painted. Be sure to press firmly along the edges of the tape to prevent paint from seeping underneath.

2 Paint over the logo with a color that is darker or more intense than the printing and the bag. Or, try white fabric paint, which in some products such as Neopaque provides better coverage than colors. Let the paint dry and apply a second and even a third coat, if needed.

3 If the printing is raised, it will always show through, especially with a flat application of one color. Various dots, spots, dashes, and lines will provide good camouflage.

Stamping

1 Use compressed sponges to create your own simple stamps. Trace around jar lids, bowls, or drinking glasses to mark circles on the sponges. Simple cookie cutters (heart, crescent) are also good templates. Cut out along marked lines. Wet the sponge so it expands, then press out most of the moisture.

2 Generously spoon paint onto a palette and use a sponge or foam brush to spread it around. If your stamping tool is soft—a sponge, rubber eraser, foam pad,

etc., press on it so it absorbs the paint. Rotate large tools for good distribution of paint. Check to be sure there's paint over the whole surface; add paint or remove a glob with a foam brush.

3 Place the stamp on the surface of the bag where you want it. Apply a little pressure. If you want an even coat of paint, twist or rotate the stamp before removing it. For a crisp stamp where the texture appears—for example, the holes of the sponge or the openings in the potato masher, lift the stamp straight up off the surface of the bag.

Stamp-a-Round Bags

Orbs: Cover tote text with lots of bright giant circles strategically placed to cover logo. Stamp with circular shapes cut from compressed sponges, plus round sponge applicators. Potato mashers add interest, too.

Folk Art: Lose the logo and let your artsy mojo grow! A flowerpot takes care of the cover-up; round sponge applicator brushes make the posies. Use fine paintbrushes to sprout stems and leaves, a cork to stamp flower centers.

Bouquet: Group blossoms over the graphics on this bag. Stamp each rotund posy with a compressed sponge; the centers were stamped with a cork. Use a thick felt-tip marker to outline and add leaves and veins.

Dip the eraser end of a pencil repeatedly into black paint to scatter polka dots all around.

Arty-Smarty Bags

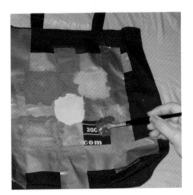

À la Paul Klee:
Emulate this artist's famous magic squares series with a multicolored grid. First, cut strips of duct tape to mask off a large square and center third of each side, as shown. Mix up a variety of paint colors, and give each exposed square two or three thin coats of a different color, letting dry after each coat. Peel off the tape, and reapply it to mask all but the center of each side of the square. Paint as before, then remove the tape. Voilà! An Amish-style Nine-Patch or a tic-tac-toe board for nickel and dime-wielding gamesters.

À la Piet Mondrian:
Mask straight-lined shapes around the logo, and paint over with several coats of white. When dry, remove the tape. Do touch-ups as necessary. Use a ruler and permanent-ink felt-tip marker to draw lines criss-crossing the painted areas. Finally, dip fine brushes into primary colors and apply several coats over one or two of the small white areas.

À la Jackson Pollack: Start by covering up the densest areas of printing, stamping with large circles or amoeba shapes cut from compressed sponges. You can also paint over the text in a color to match the bag. Now for the wild and crazy part: this is messy, so tape mini-drop-cloths over any areas where you don't want paint. Then go to town! Dab, drip and spatter paint randomly. Load up brushes with paint, and then tap the handle to flick paint onto the surface. Use sponges to absorb excessively large globs of paint, because these will take forever to dry. Avoid moving the bag until all paint marks are thoroughly dried. 🌿

Green Cats Catchall

by Susan Shie

A VISIONARY ARTIST, Susan Shie has spent many years developing a highly intuitive and spontaneous style of chronicling her life in art quilts. In applying the same process to tote bags, she first sought out a story line: "When I put the bags out to stare at and contemplate, my sweet little gray cat Ome climbed into the sewn-together bag. I grabbed the camera and started taking research pix. Then I got the idea to put

some catnip into the bag and onto the bag with open side seams. Otis, Ome's twin—but golden, not gray—came up, and the fun began." Susan documented the ensuing catnip fight on camera and on the bags themselves, with airbrushing and diary-writing. Take inspiration from her innovative process and create the most artful and personal creative expressions, as a gift to yourself, your loved ones, and the planet!

What you'll need

Dimensions: 18" x 15" x 7" deep

- Unbleached cotton canvas shopping bag; the ones Susan used are from Enviro-tote*

- Dual purpose respirator* (filters both particles and fumes)

- Exhaust fan

- Aztek Model A470 Double Action Airbrush* with all-purpose nozzle

- Compressor for airbrush, plus appropriate gauges and airlines

- Airbrush bottles with siphon lids and solid lids

- Airbrush cleaning brushes

- Ear syringes for cleaning and for adding water to paints in bottles

- Transparent airbrush paints*: black, yellow, and green (or colors of your choice)

- Basic airpen* with size 23 gauge stainless steel needle tip

- #60 paint strainer/funnel*

- Transparent black fabric paint*

*See Resources on page 61

LOW-TECH TOOLS

If you can't figure out how to use the airbrush on your own, take a class with Susan! But if that's not possible, draw, write, and paint with these items:
- a permanent marker, such as Sharpie Rub-A-Dub Laundry Marker
- fabric paints of medium consistency, such as Jacquard Textile Colors
- a stiff, flat paint brush, ideally with boar bristles

Susan says...

"It's very hard to let go and just seriously play, but you can do it, and when you do, you are freed for your own creativity."

Preparation

1 Think about your design, paying attention to what's going on around you. Make it personal. Susan suggests warming up by drawing some ideas in a sketchbook.

2 Referring to Bags Reborn, page 20, open tote bag(s) along side seams. Insert cardboard between front and back of cut, refolded shopping bag. Pin the bag by the handles on a drop cloth-covered wall. If you cannot work outside where you have access to electricity, work near a window with an exhaust fan. For safety's sake whenever using an airbrush or when heat-setting paints, wear a respirator, and run the exhaust fan on high.

3 Read manufacturers' instructions for all tools and paints and refer to them as needed. Each time you work with a new paint or color, test the airbrush or airpen on scrap fabric before working on the bag.

Airbrushing

1 Mix black paint and pour it into the airbrush paint bottle with a solid lid on it; seal closed with a cleaning rag and shake. Then, put on the siphon cap.

2 For thin lines, set airbrush to its minimal-paint setting by moving the airbrush's paint-to-air mixture adjusting wheel all the way to the left. For thicker lines, move the wheel towards the right and hold airbrush a bit further away from the fabric. Turn on the compressor and work quickly for smooth, free-flowing outlines. Working freehand, draw one or more large, simple images with airbrush. Then, if you wish, fill the open areas with large words and medium-sized motifs.

3 Place a press cloth on the right side of the bag, and with a hot, dry iron, heat-set each airbrushed area for about a minute.

Susan Shie

Wooster, Ohio
turtlemoon.com

Calling herself an outsider diary art quilt painter, Susan Shie (pronounced "shy") has been following her heart—never mind the rules—all her life, and letting her work broadcast messages of hope and healing for the earth. Beginning in 1989 and continuing for 15 years, she led an art project called Green Quilts, in which she invited other quilters to join her in making and showing pieces that express the importance of environmental balance. Her quilts are frequently juried into top forums for art and design. She shares her home with hubby James Acord, an artist whose medium is leather, as well as feline family members, and there Susan runs the Turtle Art Camps. In these intensive adult art workshops, where her mission is to have people learn to trust their intuitive impulses in making art, Susan teaches how to use airbrush and airpen, along with regular brush painting. In 2008, *Professional Quilter Magazine* designated her Teacher of the Year.

JOURNALING

What Susan Wrote About
- What my cats love to eat and do
- Names of all the cats I have had
- A grocery list for cats
- My garden
- The horse I chose won the Preakness! Yaaay!
- Fabric shopping bags for Christmas gift wrap
- The Green Quilts movement
- An earth-healing song I wrote

What You Can Write About
- Anything in your life you want to chronicle
- Things that make you happy
- Vacation highlights
- Favorite quotations and song lyrics

4 Thoroughly wash out nozzle of the airbrush and switch to an equal solution of yellow fabric paint and water. In order to have the right flow of paint for coloring in the design, move the airbrush's wheel all the way to the right. Begin filling areas with light color. Finally, switch to green; you can get several shades of green by airbrushing on top of yellow and green areas. If you are unhappy with the intensity of your painting, rinsing will lighten it without affecting the heat-set black graphics and text. When done, briefly heat-set. Clean out all the airbrush equipment before putting it away.

Using an Airpen

1 An airpen can give you crisp, dark, fine lines for your diary writing or drawing, but is tricky to use and requires lots of practice (on scrap fabric) and patience. Thin the black fabric paint with water until it is the consistency of heavy cream. Fill airpen cartridge, using a #60 paint strainer/funnel, to keep the tip from clogging. Plug in the top of the cartridge and insert it in the airpen. Always hold

Practice—but imperfect

Remember to work on scrap fabric first and aim for a smooth, even line that shows up well. But recognize that the occasional blobs and jerks add charm and character!

the airpen upright, never tipping it back. When not writing, keep airpen upright and moist, resting it in a heavy cup with a wet paper towel in the bottom.

2 To turn on airpen, plug in the small compressor that comes with it. Place airpen tip on fabric and then cover the air hole with your middle finger to force paint out the tip. To get a thin line, apply less pressure to the air hole and move the airpen faster. To get a thicker line, move the airpen slower and apply more pressure to the air hole.

3 While Susan fills all the shapes and background areas with diary writing, you can do as much or as little as you like. To avoid smearing, write in one area at a time, then let that area dry for 20 minutes, or as needed, before going on to another area.

4 When the writing is completed, heat-set with a press cloth and hot, dry iron for 5 minutes, working over the right side of the work when the fabric is thick, as with canvas. (Note: If you are working with thinner fabric, iron it paint side down over a press cloth, to protect your ironing board.)

5 Reconstruct the bags, following the how-to's in Bags Reborn on page 20.

All Natural Healthy Dog Treat
Savory Taste of Real Liver
All USA Ingredients

Only
3 Calories
per treat!

Fresh Eggs — Taste the Difference!

The incredible
edible egg!

Orange
FLAVORED GREEN TEA
NET WT 1.28 OZ (36g)

BRO

UnBeetable!

by Jean Ray Laury

FRESH, INNOVATIVE FOLK-ART has always been Jean Ray Laury's signature style. So it should come as no surprise that she applied fresh fruit and veggie motifs to a bag using a method that's like silk-screening with neither silk nor screen. And, it's easy as 1-2-3! 1—cut simple fruit and veggie shapes from freezer paper, 2—iron the freezer paper stencils onto a bag, and 3—push the paint over the cut-outs with a squeegee. Quicker than brushing or tamping! Jean explains that her squeegee "came from an auto repair shop, where it's used to spread plastic body filler over dents—never mind how I learned about this!" But you can use a couple of old credit cards as a squeegee—more fun than spending money!

What you'll need

Dimensions: 19" x 15" x 17" deep

- 1 large, natural canvas bag (This one from SewNeau*)

- Water-based textile paints: red, yellow, green, blue, brown, white (Jean prefers Versatex*)

- Fine, black permanent-ink marker

- Freezer paper and pencil

- Small, sharp scissors

- X-Acto knife and cutting mat (optional)

- At least two credit cards or hotel key cards, for squeegee

- Rubber cement or epoxy

- Stencil brush and small, tapered brush

- Recycled foam meat trays or thin aluminum pie pans, for palettes

- Spoons for paint

*See Resources on page 61

Prepare Stencils

1 Select any or all of the veggies and fruits to stencil on your bag. On tracing paper, outline the actual-size photos shown here and on the inside covers of this book, and draw lines to separate different color areas. Go over the traced lines with felt-tip marker.

2 Refer to the specifics for each fruit or veggie on page 61. For each separate stencil, cut freezer paper at least 4" to 5" larger all around than the shape. Center the freezer paper on top of a traced motif, and retrace the lines. Then, use small, sharp scissors to cut the freezer paper

Jean Ray Laury

Clovis, California
jeanraylaury.com

Whether she's making an appliquéd wall-hanging, designing a fabric collection, or silk screening, Jean Ray Laury's work is eternally fresh, irrepressibly whimsical. Since the 1960s, Jean has been at the forefront of innovative quilting and surface design. She has written over 15 books on quilting, surface design, and imagery on fabric, including *The Total Tote Bag Book,* first published in 1977—which may have been the first tote bag book ever published, and *Imagery in Fabric* (1992, reprinted in 1997). She's been awarded a Silver Star—the highest honor for a quilter, admitted to the Quilter's Hall of Fame, and one of her quilts was chosen to be among "America's 100 Best Quilts of the 20th Century."

along the traced lines. For more precise cuts, use an X-Acto knife and work on a cutting mat.

3 To make a squeegee, glue two plastic credit cards or hotel key cards together, one on top of another, making a thicker, less flexible tool. While you can use different edges to spread the paint, making more than one squeegee means you don't have to worry about getting paint where you don't want it, or thoroughly clean the squeegee before changing colors.

4 Put cardboard into the bag to prevent paint seeping through to the other side. Work with only one stencil at a time. Place the cut-out, waxy side down, where you want the fruit or vegetable motif. Apply a hot, dry iron to secure it temporarily but firmly in place. Be sure cut edges are tightly bonded to the surface of the bag. Spoon paint onto the freezer paper, at one end of the cut-out. Drag the edge of the squeegee through the paint and over the cut-out. Avoid pressing the squeegee hard against a cut edge, as it is possible to force paint under the edge, especially if your canvas bag has a coarse weave.

5 Mix paints to get a wider palette of colors. Add white to make pastels, yellow for colors like lime green and carrot orange. To blend colors, add a second color while the stencil is still in place, and the first color is still wet. Apply shading by dipping a stencil brush lightly in darker paint, tamping on a paper towel until brush is nearly dry, and then brushing over the lighter color. If you want to add highlights, make sure the underlying paint is dry, and apply the highlights with a small tapered brush.

6 When the first paint color is completely dry, remove the freezer paper stencil. If you are careful, you should be able to use a stencil several times. Add details with markers or using a small, tapered brush dipped in paint.

No such thing as a mistake!

Jean says, "If you drip paint in the wrong spot, just draw a ladybug on top of it." Or, add a stray pea, a leaf, or whatever!

7 How long each fruit or veggie takes to create is determined by the number of stencils required. With just one stencil, everything can be printed at one time. If there are several stencils, each color will have to dry before you repeat the process with another one.

8 When all painting is finished, heat-set according to the paint manufacturer's instructions.

PRODUCE: THE PERFECT MOTIF!

 Beet: Deepen red paint with a dot of blue. Squeegee red from the bottom to within 2" of the top. While stencil is in place and red paint is still wet, squeegee green from the top, blending it into the red for ¼". When paint is dry, use a tapered brush to extend the root tip with same deep red and shade the sides of beet with blue.

 Radish: Squeegee same as for the beet, but use bright red paint. Shade edges of leaves with green mixed with blue. When dry, highlight center of radish and leaves with white.

Watermelon: Mix red and white paint to make pink. Squeegee the pink flesh, then the green rind. When dry, use the tapered brush to add seeds and a marker to connect rind and flesh areas.

Cherries: Use same colors and techniques as for beet. Squeegee or brush a bit of green paint on the edge of each cherry, for a sense of dimension.

 Apples: Fruit, stem, and leaf are one cut-out. For red apple, squeegee with red; squeegee green stem and leaf. Shade sides with green. For green apple, add yellow to green paint. Add blue to green paint for stem and leaf. Shade left edge of fruit.

Carrots: Mix a little red into yellow paint to get orange. Squeegee the entire bunch, then use stencil brush to add green tops. To make individual carrots stand out, use tapered brush to add more paint to some, or use a marker to outline center carrots.

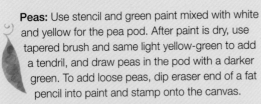 **Peas:** Use stencil and green paint mixed with white and yellow for the pea pod. After paint is dry, use tapered brush and same light yellow-green to add a tendril, and draw peas in the pod with a darker green. To add loose peas, dip eraser end of a fat pencil into paint and stamp onto the canvas.

 Corn: Cut 3 stencils: one for yellow ear, one for darker green right side of husk, and one for lighter green left side. Squeegee, shade, let paint dry, and remove freezer paper before moving on to next shape. Use a marker to draw vertical rows of corn kernels and stripes along husks.

 Mushrooms: Cut one stencil for caps, another for stems. Squeegee caps with yellow, shading with brown. Let dry, then squeegee brown or black stems. For the single portabella mushroom, use marker to outline edges and dot cap; use a tapered brush to paint underside of cap bright yellow.

Shop local to make it green! Your local quilt shop, crafts and art supply stores may carry many of the materials and tools used in this book. For further help, contact the companies listed below.

Ready-made tote bags: Enviro-Tote, Inc. (pages 20, 54), enviro-tote.com, 800-868-3224; SewNeau (pages 6, 10, 14, 18), sewneau.com

Nona Bag (page 10): Fabrics designed by Kaffe Fassett or Philip Jacobs for Westminster Fabrics, available from GloriousColor, Inc, gloriouscolor.com, 800-269-0309

What's for Dinner? (page 14): *Layered Waves* and other books, patterns by Karen Eckmeier, quilted-lizard.com; Photo-transfer: Miracle Fabric Sheets by C. Jenkins Necktie & Chemical Company, cjenkinscompany.com, 314-521-7544 ext. 22; and Printed Treasures by Milliken, Prym Consumer USA, Inc., dritz.com

Say Aloha (page 24): Organic Cotton Classic, 100% cotton bonded batting from Fairfield Processing Corp., poly-fil.com, 203-744-2090

Fine Feathered Bag (page 28): Supreme Free Motion Slider, freemotionslider. com, 239-249-0468; Wash-A-Way thread, for basting and #100 silk thread: YLI Corp., ylicorp.com, 803-985-3100; Premier Prismacolor pencils, Prismacolor.com, 800-323-0749; Tsukineko All Purpose Ink, applied with the Fantastix tool or a brush wiped dry, tsukineko.com, 425-883-7733

14-Carrot Gold (page 32): Satin cord, plastic webbing 1" wide, package of gold-toned hook fasteners, gold-toned D-rings: Jo-ann Fabric & Craft Stores, joann.com, 888-739-4120; Timtex stiff interfacing distributed by C&T, sold in 13.5" x 22" packages (2 will allow for a bag with slightly shorter dimensions) or in 10 yard bolts, 22" wide, ctpub.com, 800- 284-1114 *or* use double thickness of Pellon Peltex 1-sided fusible stabilizer, 20" wide, Pellonideas.com, 727-388-7171; Nature-fil Bamboo Batting, a blend of 50% naturally antibacterial bamboo fiber and 50% organic cotton, Fairfield Processing Corp., poly-fil.com, 800-980-8000

A Tisket, A Tasket (page 36): Lace Shopping Basket designed by Swedish artisan Marie-Louise Gustavsson. Black or white, made from polypropylene, removable polyester strap. The Container Store, containerstore.com, 888-CONTAIN (266-8246); Timtex: see 14-Carrot Gold; Handmade felt beads, Artgirlz, Artgirlz.com, 401-244-5819

Pocket Masterpiece (page 40): For additional info on Lonni Rossi Fabrics designs: lonnirossi.com, 610-896-0500; Poppy Red Hemp Fabric, fabric.com, 888-455-2940; "Paintbox" and "Petals" Collection for Andover Fabrics, andoverfabrics.com, 800-223-5678; Sulky threads and Sulky Totally Stable stabilizer, Sulky of America, sulky.com, 800-874-4115; Pellon Wonder Under fusible web #805 with paper backing, pellonideas.com, 727-388-7171; Mini Cut A Round Tool by Cheryl Phillips for making perfect circles, 2" to 8", phillipsfiberart.com, 970-874-8680; Nature-fil Bamboo Batting, see 14-Carrot Gold

Seminole Inspiration (page 44): Cherrywood Fabrics, Inc., cherrywoodfabrics.com, 888-298-0967; Fasturn Fabric Tube Turning System from Fasturn, LLC, fasturn.net, 800-729-0280

Lose the Logo (page 50) Jacquard Neopaque Starter Set—(6) 2.25oz. jars (Yellow, Red, Blue, Black, White, Magenta), Dharma Trading Co., dharmatrading.com, 800-542-5227; compressed sponges, Blick Art Materials, dickblick.com, 800-828-4548; Essentials Spouncers Set, (3) 1¼", (3) ¼", (4) ¾" sponge applicator from Plaid Enterprises, Inc., plaidcraftexpress.com, 800-842-4197

Green Cats Catchall (page 54): 3M 6000 latex free respirator from Uline. com; Aztek Model A470 Double Action Airbrush and other accessories for airbrush and airpen, Blick Art Materials, see Lose the Logo; Basic airpen with size 23 gauge stainless steel needle tip from Silkpaint, Silkpaint.com, 800-563-0074; ear wax removal syringes, check your local pharmacy; Jacquard fabric paints from Dharma Trading Co., see Lose the Logo

UnBeetable! (p. 58): Versatex paints, dharmatrading.com, 800-542-5227

Bag Basics

Here's where you'll literally bag most of the basic information you need. Hey, even though you're at the end of the book, this happens to be a great place to start!

Customize

First things first: As long as you're making the bag, make sure it'll work for you—or the lucky recipient who will be carrying it.

- Consider your mode of transportation—for car trunks or seats, make high-top bags with a loop and button, so contents won't spill. For wheelie carts, why not size your bag to fit?

- Consider your strength and tolerance for schlepping. Make smaller-sized bags if you can't cope with a ton of stuff packed into one big tote, or two same-sized bags to help you equalize the weight.

- Consider your height—no one wants a bag to drag on the ground. If you petites 5'4" and under want a large bag to carry all your stuff, shorten the handles, or stitch them on well below the rim. Tall "toters" can of course handle longer pendulum swings!

- If you like hefting tote bags onto your shoulder, consider long straps. Check out the Seminole bag; those soft corded handles are, ahhhh, so comfortable, and versatile, too.

- Think about your shopping habits and lifestyle. If you don't like to carry a purse, build just the right size pockets into your tote bag interior for carrying your wallet, cell phone, and car keys.

- Add pockets that are deep and flat for stashing lots of coupons, and narrow but easily accessible for your shopping list. My hubby, who is my resident CEO—consistently, expertly organized—appreciates a spot for a pen or pencil, too, so he can cross items off the list as he shops.

- If you'll be buying wine or some very good olive oil, why not add bottle girdles, like those on A Tisket, A Tasket on page 36?

Fabrics going green

Unless noted otherwise, fabrics listed in this book are 100% cotton, 42" wide. To conserve and save money, you can often use these helpful store cuts: Fat quarters are 18" x 22"; fat eighths are 9" x 11".

Making it green can mean . . .

. . . using what you have—upholstery samples, old polyester-cotton blends, felted wool, or artist's canvas, and of course, whatever's already in your stash!

. . . putting quilt tops, quilt fragments, quilt projects that have lost your interest, and quilt class samples to good use.

. . . repurposing items such as denim jeans, vintage dish-towels, a threadbare rag-rug or pair of faded placemats, and old tablecloths—especially ripped, flannel-backed vinyl ones or stained linens.

Before you work with any fabrics (except vinyl), pre-wash them with hot water and laundry detergent, and machine-dry them to shrink them, so future launderings won't distort the finished bag and spoil the effect. You want to avoid the possibility of mold, mildew, and dyes that bleed. Also avoid using older, weakened fibers that don't hold up under heavy-duty washing.

Canvassing the joint: cutting and stitching

If you're a quilter, apply all the good quilting habits you're already accustomed to. If you're new to sewing, enlist someone with experience to help you. Use the following:

- new, sharp, 45mm rotary blades
- good quality, comfortable fabric-cutting scissors
- 80/12 machine needles
- 50-weight sewing thread for piecing
- ¼" seam allowances—unless otherwise indicated

Working with heavy fabrics, such as canvas, denim, linen, hemp, indoor-outdoor textiles (Sunbrella is one brand name), and thick interfacings (Timtex or doubled Peltex) results in more durable totes. But with heavy fabrics, you need to change your mode of operation to avoid calluses: Rely on a 60mm rotary blade and a spring-action scissors (Ginghers makes this) to make the cut clean and easy.

When it comes to sewing through thick layers, most sewing machines—with the exception of featherweights—should stand up to the job. I prefer a 90/14 needle for heavy-duty jobs, finding that the size 16 jeans needle leaves too big a hole. And I recommend a strong thread, 40 weight on top and 50 in the bobbin for heavy-duty sewing, appliqué and quilting, and topstitching. I also love a thread that calls attention to itself: 12 to 30 weight threads, shiny rayon and variegated color-shifters.

Made from scratch

1 Determine the dimensions of the bag you want—height, width, and depth.

2 For a gusseted bag, add 1" to all desired dimensions and follow the directions for the Fine Feathered Bag on page 28.

3 For a simple, boxed-bottom bag, use the Pocket Masterpiece as inspiration. Adopt the dimensions on the cutting diagram shown on page 42, and use to make the outer bag and the lining with your own, medium- or heavy-weight fabrics.

4 For a boxed-bottom bag with tent-tucks at the bottom corners, add half the depth to the width and length. As described and shown on page 20, fold large tucks into the bottom of the adorned bag, and stitch the side seams securely.

Get a handle on it!

1 Cut handles from heavy interfacing, such as Timtex, 1" x 16"—or as desired. To cover these—or handles you've removed from a ready-made tote, cut fabric 3 times the width of each handle plus ½", and 1" longer than the length. Press raw edges ¼" to wrong side along one long side. Position the opposite, unpressed side of fabric along one long edge of handle. Wrap fabric around handle, folding raw edges ¼" over the edges of the handle and covering them with the pressed edges. Pin and topstitch.

2 As alternatives, use plastic webbing, two strands of grosgrain ribbon, curtain tie-backs, a man's necktie, wood beads threaded onto a wire, handles recycled from an old tote bag or purse, or a purchased set of handles from the notions department or craft store.

3 Stitch ends of fabric handles to the inside or outside of your bag. Either way, secure with a boxed criss-cross: a square slightly smaller than the width of the handle, divided in half diagonally in both directions.

Watch Your Bottom Line

Almost every bag in this book has a flat bottom so it can sit easily in your car trunk or stand on the cashier's belt for easy bagging of groceries. Wanna turn a flat, two-dimensional sack into a 3-D, box-bottom bag? Here's how:

Go from flat to 3-D.

1 Turn bag wrong side out and align side seam with lengthwise center of bag bottom. Note the triangular peak that forms.

2 Use a contrast-color pencil and ruler to mark the base of the triangle so it measures 4", or the desired width of the bag bottom. Pin, then stitch along this marked line, and stitch again, ⅛" away from the seam to reinforce it. Do the same thing on the other side.

3 Turn the bag right side out.

To make your tote better able to stand up and hold bottles, cans, and jars, add an insert. Use plastic needlepoint canvas, two layers of stiffened felt with fusible web in between, or Timtex, cut to the right size for the base of your bag. Leave the rigid rectangle as is, or wrap it in a fabric envelope. Encased in the same fabric as the lining, you've got a "false bottom," but a true sturdiness for your bag.

Now go shopping!

About Eleanor Levie

Eleanor Levie is a quilter, author, editor, book producer, teacher, and lecturer with a warm and wacky personality. She loves to inspire creativity, and encourage quilters to think outside the box. These passions are exemplified in all her books. Most recently, Elly was the creative force behind the best-seller, *Skinny Quilts & Table Runners* and its new sequel, *Skinny Quilts & Table Runners II.* Diverse and delightful also describe the eight volumes of the Rodale's *Successful Quilting Library* series that Elly produced, and the books *Great Little Quilts, Country Living's Country Quilts,* and *American Quiltmaking: 1970-2000,* which she authored. As a quilt historian and collector, she revels in antiques and contemporary masterpieces that break the rules and dare to be different.

Elly lives with her hubby in beautiful Bucks County, PA, where her eco-conscious lifestyle has always included shopping locally (and often!), at farm stores as well as quilt shops. A commitment to repurposing, reusing, and recycling brings Elly naturally to handmade, eco-kind totes. Having forgotten her cloth tote bags more than once, she wants to make sure that yours are unforgettable!

For quilt guild presentations and workshops, editing services, and autographed copies of this and other books, visit Elly on the web at www.EleanorLevie.com.